THE SMALL BUSINESS BIBLE

Learn How to Collect, Control, and Utilize Data and Grow sales by 63% in 60 days

Dennis M. Wilson

Cover Design by: Aljun Majo and Jefferson Balorio
Photo Credit: Kiyokazu Watanabe

The Small Business Bible: learn how to collect, control, and utilize data and grow sales by 63% in 60 days is a work of nonfiction. Nonetheless some names and persons characteristics of individuals or events have been changed to disguise some very awesome people. Resulting resemblance to persons living or dead is entirely coincidental and unintentional.

Dennis M. Wilson, author, *The Small Business Bible: learn how to collect, control, and utilize data and grow sales by 63% in 60 days*

ISBN-13: 978-1976238673
ISBN- 10 1976238676

Published in the United States by

Internetnextstep.com Smallbizdream.com

Contents

INTRODUCTION

There are so many business books out there you might wonder why you need another. A quick search for business books on Amazon yields over 2,200,000 results. That's a staggering number of books by anyone's standard. If you search 'small business books' you get, a much smaller – yet not insignificant – number of almost 260,000 choices.

You could never read all the business books ever written even if you had all the time in the world – let alone run your business. Nor would you ever want to.

But imagine if there was a book that took you on a fun and educational journey about ways small businesses have changed their futures by dramatically increasing sales with just a few small tweaks to how they approach their customers and the way they look at things.

Imagine there is a book that shares with you everything you need to know about marketing your business and succeeding in this uber-competitive world by way of some great stories and case studies.

I have been in business for myself ever since I was 10, selling pet rocks, going door to door.

If most small businesses were succeeding, then perhaps I wouldn't need to write a book. In fact, I might not need to be in business at all because nobody would need my help.

However, the sad fact is small businesses fail most of the time. According to Forbes only 50% of small businesses survive the first year and 70% the second. These are terrible stats!

Many businesses use what I call the 'hope and pray method'.

This is where they will find a great location, hire some staff, maybe even do some advertising and then sit back and wait, hoping customers will flock to their business. They try their best to be strategic but are too overwhelmed and stressed to really figure out a plan. It doesn't have to be like this.

Instead businesses need to be proactive in how they reach and retain customers. They need systems in place to attract new customers and retain old customers. They need to be deliberate in everything they do. Every small thing they do matters. In fact, it's often the small details that matter most and are key to success. It's the small but significant habits that cause a business to be successful or fail.

If businesses keep track of customers, figure out how often they buy where they come from, why they choose one business over the competition, and other data then businesses wouldn't fail at the rate they do now.

That is why I created Small Business Dream: to help entrepreneurs and business owners achieve their dreams. It's to share with you how to be successful and ultimately live the life you want while running your successful small business.

In this book, I'm going to give you actionable advice so you don't get stuck feeling overwhelmed or unable or confused. It's going to be simple and straightforward so anybody, no matter what business you are in, or what stage you are at, you can use it. I will take specific businesses and look at their situations. While you might have a completely different business, you can probably apply the principles to your situation.

This book wasn't created to be read linearly page by page. Please feel free to look at the table of contents and skip around and read the chapters you want. Come back and re-read them again. I guarantee that each time you'll get something different from them.

Everybody I talk to has a different definition of small business. We all know what a conglomerate is, but what is a small business? For some it's a solopreneur, for some it's a business less than 25 people and to others still, it is a business up to 500 employees.

The Merriam-Webster diction defines a small business as an independently owned and operated business that is not dominate in its field of operations.

I would say modestly that this definition is at the core of what is wrong with small business owners.

Why can't a small business dominate its field?

Just because it's small doesn't mean that it cannot beat its larger competition. Never in the history of business have we had a more level playing field. The internet has made it possible for anybody to be in business for themselves. Which is why small businesses are growing at an astounding rate.

Small businesses might have to be a little more creative when it comes to the way they market, sell, and produce its products and services, but that doesn't mean it's any worse than how larger companies do it.

Small businesses are the future. Conglomerates can't keep up with the level of customer service small businesses offer, nor with the fast-paced market place or with the level of specialization small business can provide.

Big business' time is up. They came to prominence last century and this new century will put them on life support. Nobody wants to be a cog in a wheel anymore. The world is too varied and people just have way too many choices for a bloated middle management. Just look at the news lately with how many department stores are filing for bankruptcy and how many malls are expected to do the same.

From carpet stores, to hair salons, to realtors and restaurants, we have assembled some amazing stories, but they all have a difference.

We lay out the roadmap. The way to do it, how they did it, and how you can do it, and whenever possible we show you the math to demonstrate how dramatic the return on investment of time and money is!

We hope you enjoy reading it as much as we have enjoyed writing and assembling it for you!

PART I: SMALL BUSINESS

WHY YOU SHOULD BE AN ENTREPRENEUR

There has never been a better time to start your own business. In fact, in the next decade, being an entrepreneur will bring more security than being an employee. We are in the middle of a great entrepreneurial boom with the number of entrepreneurs in the United States and Canada rising slowly in the 20th century.

For example, baby boomers, age 50 and above, have started an average of 3.5 companies but with millennials that figure more than doubles to 7.7 companies. This is an incredible stat that will only increase to unprecedented levels in the near future.

While running your own business may not be your dream, if you've ever considered it, hopefully this book will help you take the next step. There are no more cushy jobs anymore. No more pensions and no more unions to take care of you when you get old. The job market is shifting and the middle class is slowly disappearing. As much as we'd like our presidents and leaders to change that fact, they can't. Globalization and technology is affecting how we do business. I guarantee if you don't start your own business, you'll be left behind.

It's great to be your own boss. You don't have some higher power telling you what to do. Your future is in your own hands, and not at the whim of somebody else.

I always like to joke that as my own boss and owner of a small business I can take any Thursday afternoon off for a round of golf I want, just as long as I put in a solid Saturday to make it up.

But seriously, I believe owning a small business has some serious advantages and is easier than ever to achieve.

Online shopping is becoming more and more popular – and it isn't even close to being at its peak yet. In the future, most purchases will be online, and shopping malls will be a thing of the past. You can already see this in how many anchor tenant department stores are filing for bankruptcy and how fast Amazon's sales continue to grow.

People, especially non-entrepreneurs are going to have to move with the shifting times. Many people will lose their jobs, and be forced into entrepreneurial roles.

Today, you can start your own online business for very little capital, unlike a couple of decades ago when you needed huge amounts of money to open a storefront, to market yourself, and to hire employees. Now you just need an internet connection and you can sell to anybody and hire anybody.

Just look how many products are being sold by entrepreneurs on Facebook. You can find these same products on Amazon for 30 to 50% cheaper and it is exactly the same thing. Someone is in business and making more money with better marketing!

That said, one of the most powerful hybrids likely to emerge over the next few years will be a storefront to display products with the backroom furiously fulfilling online orders.

Small business is growing more rapidly than ever before and it's only going to become a bigger part of the overall economy. Conglomerates will still have their place but the sooner small business owners realize their power the better.

During the 2008 recession, many people were laid off or fired and as a result they became entrepreneurs. Getting downsized became a jumping off point for those who always had dreams of doing something different.

A lot of companies don't want employees any more, especially those started by millennials. They don't want to have to pay benefits.

They don't want to have to worry about slow markets. It has gotten a lot easier to just hire consultants and freelancers. Just look online where jobs and job sites are in abundance. Hiring a freelancer is only a click away. And why wouldn't companies do that instead of investing in training and managing them?

Businesses are also becoming more automated than ever before. For example, you can order your Starbucks beverage through your mobile phone and pick it up at the counter, eliminating the need for cashiers.

As a small business consultant, I just cannot help myself but to interject a quick story here to point out a SERIOUS issue a company the size of Starbucks can create for themselves as a problem without even realizing it.

As Starbucks went from a gift card to a mobile app, they did it VERY well. They didn't over think it. You opened the app, and the most likely action you would take by opening the app happened first. You saw your card and the barcode to be scanned by the barista. In 5 seconds, scanned and paid. Brilliant.

Then, as Starbucks got more faith the app was the way to go, they redesigned it. OOPS! You now have to click the pay button, which is small and to the VERY top LEFT of your screen, the hardest place to reach one handed. That then brings you a graphic of your card, and you now have to click the PAY button AGAIN at the bottom which finally brings up the bar code for the barista to scan.

Sometimes this can take 30 seconds!

Now, I am sure you have heard how upset everybody is with the lines due to mobile ordering? Imagine if they removed the 30 second wait for ½ their customers trying to pay by the app?

I have suggested to many a barista they may be able to be employee of the month by suggesting this to Starbucks headquarters. Seems the big huge sluggish companies can really mess things up, just as we stated earlier!

Ok, let's get back on track!

You can now self-checkout at your local supermarket. Low skilled jobs are getting fewer and fewer as it is becoming easier to automate more systems.

Soon robots and computer programs will be taking over for people and take many of their jobs. Robots don't need lunch breaks or vacations and they don't need feeding. They won't quit and move to a higher paying job.

Self-driving cars and even freight carrying trucks will soon eliminate the need for drivers and are just one of the many advancements to come.

Young people are seeing the necessity of being a small business owner in this rapidly changing world. Young people want more flexibility. They don't want to be stuck in traffic, commuting for an hour each way like their parents did. They want a better work-life balance.

Even if you don't want to become a full-time entrepreneur, you need the skills I will outline in this book as the job market becomes faster paced and more competitive.

COMMON CHALLENGES FACING SMALL BUSINESSES

Is it the time of year where you should be thinking about your business plan and how to move forward? What do you wish to accomplish in the coming year? How are you going to expand your business?

Wasp Barcode Technologies, an American firm, recently surveyed more than 1,000 small businesses and produced a report showing some interesting challenges many businesses face today. Over 50% of businesses say hiring is their toughest challenge, followed by cash flow. One thing is for certain, it's tougher than ever before to fight against big business and overseas companies, so we've compiled some ways to combat these difficulties.

Hiring

Every person in your operation is critical. You've probably heard the saying, 'you're only as strong as your weakest link.' It's especially true in small business. One poor performer can have major negative impact on your entire organization. That's why it's critical to hire amazing employees.

It's especially important for small businesses because, while a bigger business can bear the brunt if an employee doesn't work out, many small businesses can't. It's expensive to train and bring a new employee onboard.

According to some estimates, the total cost of onboarding can be up to 6 months of the salary of the position, and it takes an average of 30 hours to find the right person. With these challenges, it's no wonder a lot of owners try to take short cuts and hire a quick fix—a person who often turns out to be wrong for the job.

It you're planning on hiring somebody, you need to do it before it becomes critical. You don't want to be hiring staring down the barrel of a shotgun. You should block off at least an hour a day to go through resumes, do phone screening, and interviews. The other option is to hire an outside HR consultant who can help find the right person for you.

Don't forget, as a small business owner, sometimes it will seem impossible to find the money to hire an outside consultant to do something for you much more successfully than you can do it yourself. This is FALSE economy. The truth is, FIND THE CASH, as not hiring the professional at times can cost you multiple times the money you thought you couldn't find in the first place.

Finances

The number one reason small businesses fail is because they don't understand cash flow. Cash flow requires adequate planning and oversight. Owners need to keep track of incoming and outgoing cash. It's surprising most small businesses don't know where their money is going. To help create basic financial reporting you might consider using a program like QuickBooks, or even a simple spreadsheet is better than nothing. You should also create and examine a Profit & Loss statement.

While it's good to look in the past at sales reports, they don't always predict future outcomes. Most businesses don't look towards what are called Lead Measures. According to the book '4 Disciplines of Execution' these are both predictive and influential goals. For example, a Lead Measure goal could be looking at your inventory and keeping a certain bestselling item in stock.

Marketing

Marketing is key for any business, no matter how big or small. In 2017, it's going to be even more crucial as competition is going to get tougher. (And you thought that wasn't possible?) You'll need a great brand strategy to ensure you can differentiate yourself from, say, that company in China that can do it for cheaper.

We can't emphasize this enough: you need to make marketing a priority. When you start your own business, there is no guidebook on how to promote your business—not that it would do you any good with the constant changing in technology. Marketing is becoming more difficult to keep up with than ever before.

However, there are plenty of resources to help you. A lot of companies offer marketing training.

You should also read trustworthy blogs and newsletters. There are many great online resources that cater to your specific niche. Do a little digging and find out what they are.

You should create a marketing plan including your target audience and measurable goals. If you can't do it all yourself, hire a marketing company to handle your workflow for you. It's a worthwhile investment. Do your research and find an agency that fits your budget, understands your brand and will help you achieve those goals.

As a small business owner, you face many distinct challenges large corporations don't. You must be on top of your business. You must be agile. Otherwise your competition will take your clients. Focus on your advantages and leverage them in ways your competition can't.

HOW A CARPET STORE USED A SECRET WEAPON TO SUPERCHARGE SALES

There once was a little carpet store in Richmond, BC (Canada) that hired a family member, (let's call him John, name is changed to protect the awesome!) to come in and try to help with the carpet store's sagging sales.

The carpet store was one of the smallest in a larger carpet store franchise, and things just weren't going well for it. A much larger sister carpet store in the same franchise kept bringing in the big sales numbers, but his poor little carpet store just kept plodding along with very little sales growth, or improvement in profits.

Now, John joined the carpet store just to help out a bit, and he had extensive sales experience. The rumor was he could sell refrigerators to Eskimos. (Canadian joke eh!)

For months and months John tried and tried, but just couldn't change the carpet store's pitiful sales numbers.

He had a friend named Dennis M. Wilson who owned a small business consulting company, that offered to provide John with a "secret weapon" to turn sales growth ON and increase profitability FAST!

During the conversation, Dennis told John he could save him time in the sales process during his day as well.

Low on belief, but trusting of Dennis, John agreed to learn more. He didn't tell his family he was doing this, just in case the "secret weapon" didn't work.

So, what was the secret weapon he was offered?

Sorry, not so fast! Let me start by telling you about the magic that happened to sales because of this "secret weapon"!

The carpet store franchise is quite organized as far as giving recognition for both the stores, and to their salespeople for being outstanding.

John went from nearly a year of obscurity in the carpet store franchise sales rankings, never once making the top of anything, working in a carpet store in the smallest category that also never made it to any of the top performer lists, even against the carpet stores of the same small category, to accomplish some truly amazing things.

John became the top selling sales rep in all the top-level carpet stores, and the other salesperson in the carpet store who also secretly used the 'secret weapon' became 2nd! This was within 60 days of employing it on the retail floor of their carpet store!

The store became one of the TOP 3 performing carpet stores in the chain! NOT just in their weight group!

How?

What was this secret weapon?

It's much simpler than you might think.

Small Business Dream Sales and Marketing Automation with CRM
We have a salesperson in a carpet store that saw the power and got Small Business Dream for himself to help him earn a higher commission check, he didn't know what he was getting himself in to

Check out the video at twt.bz/carpet

It comes from thinking outside the box, and doing something many would say is not recommended as a carpet store sales strategy!

The "secret weapon" was Small Business Dream, a mobile and web application. Not just any old mobile or web application, but a mobile application AND a web application. Quite a simple yet comprehensive sales, marketing and email automation mobile CRM software suite.

John set about to secretly increase the carpet store's sales using Small Business Dream, he spent a few days tweaking and playing to establish a good sales method, funnel, flow, and follow up including comfortably getting carpet store customers to take a short survey and agree to give their email address to get more information and stay in touch with John and the carpet store.

He had configured several email auto-responder follow up series to follow up with people interested in particular items like Carpet, Hardwood Flooring, or Linoleum etc.

A week later, John had about 35 contacts who had gone through his simple survey. He had automated emails based on their chosen flooring interests triggered based on what they indicated their interest was in the survey questions.

John did NOT give his mobile phone to the prospect to attempt to fill in the details themselves, he filled in the Survey for them to keep it frictionless. When the carpet store was too busy, he had them fill in a small 1/8 size piece of paper asking the same things and collecting their data to enter into the mobile CRM later.

The following week he had made 3 sales he knew he never would have chased or followed up with without the sales automation due to the small order size or feeling the person wasn't serious about purchasing. (This is a critical error of any salesperson, never prejudge, we ALL know it as sales professionals, but we all still do it! More on that later!)

More exciting was suddenly a lot of communication had opened up by email and instant messaging vs. needing to try to contact each other on the phone by voice. Quick and efficient.

He started to use Small Business Dream to follow up on in store visits, measures, installations, and the whole 9 yards of the carpet business. Suddenly John was the "Go To" guy in the carpet store for anything, as the carpet store's paper based systems were so impossible to use, and finding quotes or previous paperwork was close to impossible.

Due to the Small Business Dream, mini CRM John was using, all of that info was at his fingertips, in real time. He even got calls on his days off to answer carpet store questions as only he could get the answer quickly in his mobile app!

His carpet store sales were up year on year and month on month, from the very first month that the app was secretly employed. The carpet store owner couldn't figure it out.

Fun things started to happen!

A guy walked into the carpet store on John's day off and says to the other rep on the floor that day: "I don't remember who I talked to over a month ago when I got a quote for $2900 worth of flooring from your store, but he has followed up with me by email constantly to see where I am at. Please sell me that flooring!!" So cha ching... John on his day off closes a $2900 deal at 9% for an unexpected extra commission of $261 and decides to have steak and lobster for dinner!

As things progressed, John kept talking to Dennis, and Dennis suggested John push the email follow ups further than the few weeks that John had done so far. Dennis suggested a 3 month and a 6 month follow up email to be sent on each category.

John wasn't sure, and put up some resistance, saying nobody in Carpet or Flooring waits 3 or 6 months to buy, so it's a waste of time. Dennis suggested it was free to add a few emails, would only take 20 minutes to write and upload them, so what did John have to lose?

Dennis also knew in Vancouver, BC, Canada and many cities around the world, a building permit could take 4 to 6 months or more in some cases to obtain. If the renovation or new construction needing the carpet or flooring was delayed due to the permit process, it was logical a 6 month later follow up could possibly yield results. And guess what?

IT DID!

Within a week of adding the 3 and 6-month automated follow up emails to the series, a customer came into the store asking where the guy that kept emailing him was. John felt like hiding, the guy seemed angry. The other sales rep, not wanting to be mistakenly singled out immediately pointed at John and said, it must have been John!

The guy walked up to John, re-introduced himself, and said he was ready to go, the permits had finally come in on that $14000 carpet job. Almost ½ of John's monthly quota for the very slow month that the sale came in! $14,000 x 9% = $1260!

He then also said very clearly John was not the cheapest carpet store he got a quote from, but he was the only salesperson still following up, and he felt if the service before the sale was so great, the service after must be excellent.

So, John simply took a little time to get prospect and customer data and put it into a mobile CRM, by actually taking the customer's time to do it right in front of them. Many say you shouldn't do that.

John's experience? Customers loved the follow up, they loved they got emails from John which reminded them of questions they had to ask, and could easily ask by email or instant message like Skype or SMS/Text message, or Facebook Messenger vs. having to phone John.

The carpet store had a "Truckload Sale" on area carpets one weekend. Imagine the family's surprise when, by the time they got in, the truck was empty as John had sold every single one by sending out a simple email blast to the 620 or so previous customers, and existing prospects with a time limited sale offer for that truckload of area rugs.

Now John's carpet store is rabidly awaiting the Small Business Dream (www.smallbizdream.com) add on app called myCarpetStore to allow their customers and prospects to connect directly to them, and receive updates, specials, and follow up directly to their mobile device by push notification in addition to email!

DATA = POWER

DATA in a usable format, and the creativity on how to use it = Sales and PROFIT GROWTH.

What do you have to lose?

Furniture Stores, Industrial Supply, Electronics stores, Shoe Stores, Hair Salons, Spa's, Financial Planners, Real Estate agents, and the list goes on and on who could benefit with similar simple strategies.

HOW TO STAY AHEAD OF THE COMPETITION

Each time companies miss out on a marketing opportunity, they've unwittingly given their competitors a better chance to gain the initiative in the marketplace. To win in a fiercely competitive environment, businesses must learn to look for missed opportunities and seal the gaps in their marketing strategies.

Some of the most common missed opportunities are surprisingly simple but can have a huge impact in promoting businesses. It also shows with a little bit of creativity and by being sensitive to our customers' needs, we can create meaningful connections and move our products and services closer to them.

How Businesses Are Taking Advantage of Customer Data

Businesses that have been around for quite some time have the advantage of being able to track customer activity and see the whole picture of the history of what's really gone on with their sales and marketing strategy. This enables them to map out their next strategy based on current trends and make some slight adjustments for future customer engagements.

Customer data allows businesses to identify weak spots, i.e. missed opportunities, and use that information to gain an advantage in the marketplace. Most of these marketing opportunities are common but have the potential of improving sales significantly.

Startup companies can also take advantage of big data from

another source such as Google Analytics, AdWords, Facebook Ads, and Facebook analytics along with other free data tracking tools. To really understand and appreciate customer data for marketing solutions, a good CRM (customer relationship management) service or application should be in place.

Practical Marketing Solutions

Missed marketing opportunities are essentially like blind spots; they've been there all along but we can't see them through our peripheral vision. Marketers can get so overwhelmed with the numbers they often overlook the most basic, yet very effective marketing strategies that have already stood the test of time.

These marketing opportunities include:

Social Media Marketing – although not generally regarded as a primary marketing tool for most small business types, can still contribute to your overall marketing efforts. Maybe even as much as 20 percent. Remember, timing is key here. On average, it takes three to five hours for a status update or post to reach peak activity, followed by a steady decline in viewer's interest. Be careful what time you post, OR use a scheduling tool like hootsuite.com to set things in advance to post at your audiences peak viewing time.

Peak hours will differ from country to country and marketers will have to experiment with different posting times. The old practice of buying 'likes', 'fans', and 'followers' had already lost its usefulness.

Social media marketers are now re-focusing their efforts in sharing timely and relevant information, upcoming events, contests as well as collecting data from fans and followers (contact information, hobbies, interests, etc.) for other marketing strategies. Thus extending their reach through multi-channel marketing (particularly email and mobile marketing).

Cross-selling & Upselling – This is usually practiced during the final stages of the buyer's journey in the sales pipeline or during follow-ups and education with regular customers.

Cross-selling and Upselling allows you to get as much as an additional 10 to 30 percent increase in revenue. It opens more options for buyers and potential customers, especially those product or services related to their purchase which they may have missed or left out unintentionally.

For instance, your clients have shown interest in buying carpets. You may suggest buying a carpet cleaner along with the carpet to save more money on carpet cleaning services.

Another example is a B2B business situation like selling office supplies to your customer. You could suggest personalizing some items (pens, notepads, etc.) with their company logo or brand name at just a small additional cost.

Maintaining customer loyalty for repeat purchase/service and referrals helps with customer retention which allows your company to save 5 to 10 times the marketing expenses compared to constantly having to look for new customers.

In fact, existing customers account for 65 percent of the average company's income. Businesses are now stepping up on improving customer retention and are starting to cut down on advertising expenses and promotional ventures.

More emphasis is now given to customer loyalty since this is less expensive to maintain and has the potential of producing leveraged income through customer referrals. In order to achieve this goal, they also need to increase their marketing capabilities through sales and marketing automation to cope with the growing number of prospective and existing customers.

Mobile Marketing – Recent statistics reveal as of 2016, mobile users have grown to 4.61 billion. That's more than half of the world's total population. Missing out on this one means giving away a large portion of potential customers to your competitors. Mobile marketing has already been employed by a lot of companies successfully to promote their brand, collect customer information, and maintain customer relationship.

One great example is through their use of free mobile applications like Small Business Dream (smallbizdream.com you can use it for free up to 2000 communications per month) on mobile platforms such as Google Play and iTunes which allow companies to collect important relevant information about mobile users. Businesses can also employ mobile CRMs to communicate with their customers and prospects on the go.

Another advantage of mobile marketing is it gives small business owners the ability to offer an app to customers and prospective customers. The owners can then send push notifications directly to their customers' mobile devices with Small Business Dream and their associated "My" series of apps. MyRestaurant, MyCarpetStore, MyLawyer, MyClothingStore etc.

Improving the company's visibility – Some of the 'old-school' marketing strategies are still as effective as today's modern marketing approach. This is especially true with brand awareness. However, instead of spending hundreds of dollars on posters, print ads, and billboards, you can give little items with your personalized logo, brand name, or website as giveaways to your loyal customers and on-site visitors.

Things like pens, golf pencils, umbrellas, wristbands, caps, t-shirts, and other knickknacks are inexpensive yet effective marketing tools which can be used to promote your business. It doesn't cost too much, but you'll be surprised how even simple things like these can help endear your customers to your business.

Other ideas include coasters and tent cards if you're into local restaurant business, or perhaps giving a mint or two with your personalized packaging as a way of saying 'Thank you,' to your valued customers.

It only takes a little bit of creativity and keeping yourself abreast with the most recent marketing ideas and tools to stay ahead of the competition. The key is to never stop looking for more opportunities, because if you do, your competitors will do their best to catch up to you.

It pays to remember one important rule in life as it is with business: "In life there is no security; there's only opportunity."

HOW AN OBSCURE RESTAURANT BECAME A MASSIVELY PROFITABLE DOWNTOWN SENSATION

It all started in Vancouver a few years ago. A restaurant owner opened a Japanese-Style Korean barbeque franchise from Japan in Vancouver.

The small business restaurant owner selected the location, a space that was way too big in the eyes of all the restaurant owners and professionals in Vancouver, and a place where time after time, restaurants had failed to succeed in the very same space.

You see, the space was much too big for such an obscure chain restaurant doing food and drinks "normal" Vancouver people may not be able to relate to. Or so the "experts" said.

The location was bad, impossible to see, and too far back from the road, almost subterranean. Parking all around the area was also very expensive.

You see, it just couldn't work. Unless the small business owner had some kind of a secret weapon.

You could almost hear the little engine that could saying, "I think I can, I think I can, I think I can".

Now a secret weapon the small business owner surely did have! So secret they could hide it right in plain sight and have no other restaurant owners copy them.

It was so simple most restaurant owners would actually argue is not only unnecessary, but possibly even not to be tolerated by restaurant patrons.

Genius, yes. But ... frowned upon? Maybe.

The secret weapon was not really a hard thing to do, but it would take some time, training, effort, and a possibly even have a small cost.

You see, it would be hard according to most restaurant owners, as someone would have to be made responsible to do it right. One of your already overworked restaurant staff, who has no time at all when it is busy, may have to add a step to their job.

Of course, as a restaurant or small business owner, this is always difficult, as you wouldn't want to put your staff out with a work task they might not like or feel comfortable with. Or worse yet, pay some money to outsource it. You see it just won't work, so most restaurants never even bother.

Let's also not forget the fact almost nobody in the restaurant industry uses this very simple secret weapon, so it must be a bad idea. You as an entrepreneur, restaurant and small business owner should probably stop reading this book right now as the Secret Weapon is something really simple and silly and you likely won't like it or believe it.

This obscure restaurant, did the hard work of setting up this Secret Weapon for only about the first 3 months of their existence.

Then they reaped the rewards of its awesome power for YEARS to come...

They were busy, well, actually lined up almost constantly for the following two years and even to this day, just by utilizing over and over this very simple secret weapon they took the time and care to set up.

It likely cost them less than $250 to set up. It likely costs them under $100 a month to maintain.

They have now opened another location in Vancouver, and they implemented the same secret weapon they started building in location 1 for location 2. Now the 2nd location has been packed since opening day.

Ok, enough of the suspense. What is the Secret Weapon this restaurant has so successfully employed?

DATA! Yep, simple data.

Well, I guess it's not just data, it is data they collected, and now utilize almost once a week.

So let's take a look at how they implemented and utilized this secret weapon called "data".

They collected their data in an old school fashion, and we suggest this is always at least one necessary data collection method to all of our clients.

Yes, we know there are iPads, and Surfaces, and tablets, and iPhones and Android devices and all this smart technology, but sometimes old school is better for many of your restaurant guests. YES you should have a QR code on a tent card on the table and offer people to join your mailing list by filling in a simple survey from their smart phone. Some will. You could also do Coasters! Coasters are just like business cards that can be pondered at the table and even taken home.

YES you should have a very short URL to redirect to your same survey/data collection landing page for those who prefer this way.

YES you could suggest they just give their Twitter name, Instagram name, Facebook name, or email address.

YES you should ask them to follow you on Facebook.

BUT…

This company didn't do any of those things for the first 3

months.

They simply gave out a small 1/8 of a page mini survey/feedback paper to each person at the table with the bill.

They offered that all who joined the newsletter would be in a monthly draw for a $100 gift certificate.

They started with just a random pen left at the table to fill in this overly photocopied ugly piece of paper, that wasn't even cut straight (darn hard to get good help in a restaurant!).

Then they 'upped their game' and gave out a golf pencil branded with the restaurant name. Customers were even encouraged to take it home if they liked.

Then the magic happened.

They actually did something with the information! Someone was responsible to actually enter it into a CRM type sales automation system like Small Business Dream.

Check out the video at twt.bz/restaurant

They likely used the simplest one around, or who knows, maybe they simply used Outlook.

All that matters is, they took action. They made it someone's job to enter this data nightly, or who knows, maybe they paid a subcontractor to do it. And yep, I'm sure many of the surveys had hard to read email addresses, and I'd bet the bounce rate was out of this world. By the third month, I bet half or more were duplicates so they were wasting time. But they kept entering.

Right from the first week of collecting this data, they sent out the first email. Showing off specials during certain times of day, or Monday was all day Happy Hour with $9.99 pitchers of beer at the time, ALL day Monday. Within weeks Mondays were packed and pretty soon, every day was full to capacity.

They didn't sweat that many of the emails couldn't be used because they were illegible. They didn't worry their survey paper looked awful. They didn't worry their staff didn't feel comfortable handing out the survey. They didn't worry their pencils were taken home more often than not. They just continued to TWEAK their secret weapon! They continued to use their secret weapon and they continued to be full to capacity, night after night.

They opened another location, rinse and repeat. Imagine if they had an even more robust secret weapon. One that would have taken away some of the cost and time by giving patrons options like mentioned above:

1. An iPad at the bar or front desk to have people join the mailing list while they waited for a table.
2. Taking the survey by QR code
3. Taking the survey by simple URL
4. Taking the survey by submitting a direct message on Twitter, or a mention on twitter.

They continue to be a booming success, month after month, year after year, while restaurants in better locations, with better themes, and better menus, and better parking, continue to fail. Not one of the failures employed the 'secret weapon'.

Now the story gets better! This great Korean Barbeque Japanese restaurant went a step further.

They started a loyalty program with an actual member card. Customers got points for eating there, and they could then redeem the points to get $25 OFF their meals once they had enough points.

Again, back in the day, the waiter/waitress had to take your card, disappear into the back, likely login to some system that allowed them to track your purchase, and how many points you had, and notify you manually when you had enough.

They continued to evolve, they continued to add power to their secret weapon.

The loyalty program became connected to their POS terminal. The customer receipt now told you where you were at for your point balance each visit. The customer could email in a picture of their receipt if they forgot their card, and it was someone's job to match it up and credit the customer. Goodness me, what a terrible thing to make a staff member do when they are so busy!

By now I think you are starting to see this company had a bigger secret weapon than just their data, they had the determination to make it happen instead of making excuses for why it may be too hard, or the staff may not like it.

Then they upgraded their secret weapon again! They invested in a simple mobile app.

This now allowed people to join them for the purpose of getting updates as an app, and of course we all know a mobile app sends out push notifications instantly vs. an email mailing list taking some time to send once it gets large. This allowed their message to be received in real time, and not end up in a spam folder, or ignored by a millennial who only looks at their email once a week, if that.

Then they upgraded the weapon again. The entire loyalty program was now contained in the mobile application! You could literally redeem your points for something free in front of the waitress and it was brought to you. Now instead of waiting till you had $25 built up, you could redeem for even a $5 item. The patrons responded, and continue to respond, packed full night after night, and even have a very healthy lunch crowd.

July 24, 2019

draw

$30 Health Check for 10 people

⇓

put name. age.

Some Questions on dementia

⇓ location

Send $30 Health Check opportunity

OK to send a Newsletter?

⇓

free for member for HMS

members benefit

three [illegible] trial

HAPPY HOUR FOR YOUR RESTAURANT PUB OR BAR, A DISASTER WAITING TO HAPPEN?

Happy Hour, Tappy Hour, Appy Hour, regardless of your restaurant or bar type, whether you serve alcohol or not, you may benefit from implementing a Happy Hour.

It is a common fear of restaurant and bar owners worldwide Happy Hour will reduce their revenue by taking their regular customers and having them eat or drink at a discount during restaurant Happy Hour periods.

As common as this thinking is, in most cases it's simply not true. The occasion where it can be true and you must be careful, is in the case of a restaurant that never runs at capacity, even on its busiest days, in other words an unsuccessful restaurant just barely getting by, or even losing money.

If you are in this situation, it might hurt your restaurant a little bit in the short term, but it can also be the thing sparking your restaurant to being busier and growing your restaurant's customer list. You need to know why your restaurant is not busy. If your food or service is bad, Happy Hour strategies will NOT help you.

Check out the video at twt.bz/happyhour

There are essentially three ways to increase sales in a restaurant, bar, or pretty much any business;

1. **Get More Customers**

By having and promoting a restaurant happy hour, your existing customers are much more likely to bring people they know to your

establishment. Treat their guests right at your restaurant or bar's happy hour and you can retain a new customer.

Want maximum bang for your happy hour bucks? Make sure you are using a mini CRM (Customer Relationship Marketing) tool like Small Business Dream to collect all your customers' data, and the myRestaurant mobile app to allow direct push notification communication with your new restaurant customers you gained from happy hour.

2. **Increase average restaurant customer's purchase**

By putting your higher margin items at a discount like special drinks, or premium beer, or new appetizer items, you're getting people to step out of their regular restaurant or bar purchasing patterns to try some of your premium items. This can lead to higher average checks when they return to your restaurant outside of happy hour.

3. Sell more often to each customer.

By having new restaurant customers come to check you out at a discount, if you have a CRM in place helping you with your sales and marketing automation tasks like letting them join your newsletter, or specials updates letter, you will have the ability to have them come back to your restaurant or bar due to your direct invitation with an offer that is NOT happy hour.

Done right, with the purpose of building your restaurant customer list to re-market to, Happy Hour can hardly ever get your restaurant or bar in trouble.

Interestingly enough, the busier your restaurant or pub is during your peak hours, the more you can increase ongoing restaurant sales by having a happy hour! Think of it as bribing people to get their data to remarket to them.

If you can move 10% of your customers to come before 6 pm, having them out by 7:30 pm or 8 pm in the case of a restaurant, it allows you to pick up a few more reservations or walk-ins you may have turned away due to being full.

This is a massive boost to your bottom line if your restaurant can benefit from this. There is also a savings to your labor costs, and a benefit to your staff.

As many restaurants employ part time staff, whether you schedule them 5 hours or 6 or 7 makes little difference to the staff member, other than the positive of they get more hours and possibly don't need to work two part-time jobs.

Do your job right, and in a tipping economy, you can even earn more in the tip pool.

There are a number of things you can do to really multiply the advantage of your restaurant or bar's Happy Hour:

1. Collect restaurant customer data with a tent card on the table offering them to join your newsletter for special offers
2. Like you on Facebook,
3. Follow you on twitter,
4. Follow you on Instagram etc.
5. A QR code can be fun and easy printed on your tent card,
6. Make sure you have a super simple URL using a URL shortener so customers can easily enter the URL to be taken to your newsletter signup page.
7. Have a draw for a $100 gift certificate for any new people who subscribe to your newsletter
8. Offer a very simple and inexpensive appetizer (nuts, edamame, chips) for any who like your Face- book page, and check in.

Once you have built your restaurant customer list safely in your sales and marketing automation software, you can really start to reap the rewards of your Happy Hour endeavor by filling your restaurant at will on a slow day, by simply emailing or sending a push notification out with a special offer for those who come on the slow day at the slow time!

Don't forget you must amplify the results of your restaurant, bar, or pub happy hour by employing a mini-mobile CRM sales and marketing automation tool and mobile app for your customers like Small Business Dream

Do you know why you should have your restaurant customer data?

The reason you want to collect this data and build a mailing list is to eliminate sales vacancy. What is sales Vacancy? An empty table when you have staff to cover it is sales vacancy, and sales vacancy is almost p u r e profit if you are at least breaking even on your current sales volume.

Once you have this data collected, you can literally fill your restaurant on a slow day with thc click of a few buttons. Let's say you know Monday nights are often slow, you could send an email to your list offering 2 for 1 appetizers during the slowest period to bring people in. This is much more effective than a sign out front, as it would be seen by all your customers, not just the ones that walk by. Restaurant Owners customer data worth a minimum $26.65/ per person a year in sales! This story will share details on how to achieve this.

You could offer drink specials or have a happy hour you announce with an email blast and or push notification. Want to really ramp up sales? Send out any specials you have new this week in your weekly newsletter, and most importantly, a few you will take off the menu at the end of this week.

The funny part about this technique is it creates urgency and scarcity at the same time, making it much more likely someone will book to come and see you THIS week, vs. later or when they get around to it.

This leads to increased sales frequency which is a fantastic sales growth hack. What if you could get each customer to come back to your restaurant an extra 2 or 3 times per year. Make them come every 3 weeks vs. the natural ever 4 or 5 or 6 they normally come. Maybe that will increase your profits?

Small Business Dream allows you to utilize sales automation and marketing automation with a simple survey on paper, or as we explain later in this chapter with a few other creative and more automated methods. We recommend doing all these things at once for maximum speed of sales growth.

A paper survey is a simple 1/8 piece of paper given out with the bill to each person at the table by your wait staff. Include as many golf pencils (can buy at any office supply shop for a few cents each, or better yet order them with your restaurant name on them and let people "steal" them) as you give surveys to keep the process easy.

Ask for their name and email address, and how they liked you on a scale of 1 to 10. Food, service, ambiance. Ask them if they want to be on your mailing list, and offer something for them to give up their data and be on your mailing list. Mailing list lets us send you great offers and update you on menu changes etc., and 'bribe' them by saying they will be in draw to win a $100 gift certificate each month drawn from all new newsletter subscribers.

You have the option to do the data entry from the paper yourself, or you can use our automated transcription service to do it for you.

Let's do some simple math on what this data is worth to your annual sales in your small business restaurant as a restaurant owner.

If you have customers an average of 1 time per month, and these techniques we are describing can get them to come once every 3 weeks as your restaurant is now top of mind, and they get wonderful updates from you with specials, or notification of things going off the menu, or time limited specials going onto the menu, watch what happens.

Let's say you have only 1,350 people in your data base. A restaurant as small as 25 seats should easily have this within 3 months of collecting data.

If you have 25 seats at 60% occupancy on average and say 40% are new customers vs. repeat after month one. The math goes like this.

Twenty-five seats x 30 days in a month = 750 people in 1

month on your mailing list.

In the second month, 750 x 40% = 300 new people on your mailing list and each month thereafter.

In 3 months, you would have 1350 people on your mailing list.

Let's say only 60% were repeat type customers that come on average 1 time per month. That gives us 810 people.

Let's say your average bill is only $25. Your annual sales from this would be 810 x $25 x 12 (months in year) = $243,000/year.

If you now had them come back an average of once every 3 weeks, what happens?

810 x $25 x 17.33 (52 weeks in a year divided by 3 weeks average visit to get how many times per year they come) = $350,932.50!

That is a 44% increase in sales, at little or no cost to you! As you know, one of your biggest expenses is getting a new customer!

Still not convinced on the value of having your customer data?

If we look at the sales increase, divided by how many pieces of data you have, it will surprise you.

In one year, you would have collected 750 + (300 x 11) = 4050 pieces of data. Your sales increase was $350,932.50 – $243,000 = $107,932.50. If you want to consider that you only have 1350 pieces of data, that means each customer email was worth $79.95 to you. If you want to consider you had the 4050 pieces of data, each customer email was worth $26.65!

So, is it worth a bit of effort if the worst-case scenario is each piece of data you collect is worth a minimum of $26.65 to you?

Now you've seen the importance of collecting your customer data, let's look at additional ways you collect it to even further grow your sales!

You have the option to do the data entry from the paper

yourself or you can use our automated transcription service to do it for you.

One thing the little restaurant did not do, but you may want to consider in addition to the paper survey, is a fish bowl draw. Simply put a glass fish bowl at your front counter with a sign saying drop in your business card for the chance to win a $100 gift certificate each month, or a free lunch or whatever offer you feel you can afford to give to new subscribers to your list. Make sure you have some survey forms beside the fishbowl for anyone who missed them at the table and wants to fill one out.

Make sure you say on your sign that they will be added to your mailing list. Again you can transcribe the cards yourself, or use our built in human transcription service to do it for you.

Another tactic is to get a tent card made for each of your tables that displays a QR code and a short URL leading to a mailing list subscription page, or even a survey if you want to learn more about your customers. (this is another tool included in the Small Business Dream suite)

Get coasters printed with the information if you don't want the cleaning maintenance or to give up the table real estate of a tent card.

Collect newsletter subscribers from your website if you have one, and if you do not have one, get one! It does not need to be super fancy, but you do need at least a basic website!

It is simply amazing how many restaurants do not have their own website, but just rely on the YELPS of the world to do it for them.

This is bad for your restaurant business. You should have your own website so these other sites can link to it, this allows you to control the narrative a bit more, as your message how you want it to be seen is available to the public, to offset any negative reviews you get. It simply allows people to decide if the negative news is justified or not.

Without your own website, your potential customers have no choice but to form all opinions from the other sites that are collecting data and comments on your restaurant business.

Small Business Dream can be your simple website if you do not have one. No additional costs it's just one of the integrated tools in our Sales Growth Suite.

From your current website, or the one you set up in Small Business Dream you can direct people straight to your newsletter signup page, amplifying your in-store efforts by building a list of those who have not yet visited you, or saving data entry time/cost of those who join your list on their own.

Now you know the value of one piece of data is $26.65, you can see that you have no excuse to not get going on this asap as the payback is fast and huge.

Depending on your type of restaurant, and if you take reservations or not, there are a lot more tools in Small Business Dream that can benefit you.

Should you be a restaurant that takes reservations, imagine the power of having this data, including a phone number you take when the reservation is placed.

You can now track customer preferences, like for example, what wine they ordered last time, or what their food preferences or allergies are. Does it take a bit of work to collect this data? Of course! With $26.65 being the lowest return on each piece of data, it would just get better and better as you learn more and more about your customers!

A full mini CRM and mobile CRM is also included in Small Business Dream, which includes a very powerful contact manager that you can use for collecting and recalling this data.

Finally, the big elephant in the room: Social Media!

The restaurant that could, had a very cool strategy to build its Facebook followers. They offered a small appetizer that was super easy to prepare, low labor cost, and able to be done in advance. In their case they used Japanese Edamame, or soy beans. They made literally a micro portion, about ¼ of the size of the portion you got if you ordered it from the menu, served it in a funky container which made it seem special and not so small, and offered it free if you checked in and liked their Facebook page.

We would recommend you also do this for Twitter, yes, we know many think it is dying, but it still has some advantages, as Facebook has now made it very hard to communicate with your fans without paying. Only about 2% of your page likes ever see your posts organically in Facebook now. That said, it can be very cost effective to do an advertising campaign only to your fans with Facebook.

The advantage of Twitter is it can still go viral. Small Business Dream has great Twitter and other social media tools built in to its suite to help you manage these lists and posts.

Your social media campaign is most effective if it always pushes people to join your mailing list. We know it sounds old fashioned but a good email list is still worth a fortune to your business. Keeping up with social media can make you seem more relevant and cool, so doing both with the purpose of ultimately building your list is a very effective strategy.

So, are you ready to Rapidly Growth your restaurant sales?

ARE YOU READY TO IGNITE YOUR REAL ESTATE COMMISSIONS?

I want to start with my own short story about my real estate, real estate agent, and realtor experience, and please understand that I'm not saying real estate agents and professionals are all as bad as the ones I seemed to have found, but wow, do I think there may be some room for improvement! I used a real estate agent and bought eight rental properties in a period of about 18 months. You may be surprised to know but all 8 were with different realtors.

There is a simple rule I have with most things sales related. If I do not get properly followed up with, I go to the next real estate agent or salesperson who may actually have enough respect of our relationship to follow up not just up to the sale, but after it.

If you can believe it, even knowing I was buying cash flow positive rental properties that were cash flow positive, and I had a budget to buy 7 or 8, not one single real estate agent followed up after the initial sale! All my realtors were very good at following up until they made the sale and got paid their real estate commission.

AFTER the Sale, not a "hello, are you happy with the place I helped you buy?", not a "hey didn't you say you were looking for a few more cash flow properties in the area, well I found a few that may work for you", not a happy birthday, not even an "I hated working with you don't call me again".

REALTOR RADIO SILENCE!

Check out the video at twt.bz/realestate

This got me thinking the other day about how cool it would be to see just how SmallBizDream.com may help a real estate agent make larger commissions and reduce a lot of busy work.

We know for certain the biggest mistake we see realtors make is lack of follow up. The 2nd biggest mistake realtors make is the WRONG follow up!

In a realtor's world, there are 3 occasions to follow up.

The first occasion for follow up is after your first contact at a business networking event or other meeting place even if the person may not need your services immediately. Most realtors are HORRIBLE at this type of follow up and thus spend a lot of time and effort generating new "leads" as they ignore the ones they already have but haven't cultivated.

Just because someone is not ready to engage you now, doesn't mean without proper sales automation and some out of the box thinking, you can't be following up with them and moving the relationship forward.

You should get creative in your follow up to get referrals from these prospects and eventually their business when they are ready to buy or sell a home.

The key to this type of follow up is CREATING VALUE for them in all your follow up communications. If you just hit them over and over asking for referrals or for them to use you, you aren't doing it right!

If you just drop them onto a canned system you bought that just keeps hammering them with information on sales in their areas, expect them to remove themselves from your list AND YOUR LIFE!

Sending IN-APPROPRIATE follow up is even MORE DAMAGING than not following up at all.

If they are NOT ready to buy or sell and have made this clear, why would they care about values in their neighborhood?

So how do you "create value" in some email follow ups for such a cold prospect?

I started to think about myself as a home owner, the cool things I learned over the years as far as maintaining a property and how it affects the properties resale value. I imagined how happy I would have been with my real estate agent if they took the time to give me some after care on my primary residence, OR on my rental properties.

So how do you "create value" in some email follow ups for such a cold prospect?

How about an offer to put them into a Home Maintenance Reminder system?

Want to make this concept even MORE powerful, get some basic information about the home they live in now, so you can send them Home Maintenance tips specific to the Type and AGE of place they live in now.

The key to success in today's world is making sure any automated follow up you do is VERY specific to your customers' needs, vs. generic for everybody.

Getting (and keeping) your real estate business ahead of the pack in an insane market can be a massive and daunting task. All aspects of your marketing game need to be 'on point', because the competition for your potential client's hard-earned dollar is fierce.

Gone are the days when all you had to do was make sure that your face was on the side of every bus, and underneath the butts and backs of those waiting for them. This is a new era.

Escalated real estate values mean that you're going to have to put in 'extra time' and effort to getting your name and your reputation in front of those looking for your services. And there's no better way to do that, than by staying top of mind, by using the tools that were built for just this reason.

Check out the video at twt.bz/realtor

Adding a newsletter component is a given, in order to stay in touch on even a very basic level, but what about staying in touch on the fly? I mean, how often do you look to your cell phone for information before you sit down at a desktop or laptop computer?

Yup. I'm talking about mobile marketing tools for your real estate business. It's like ramping up your newsletter campaign, keeping your customers in the loop by way of mobile. It's marketing at the touch of a button.

Even though you're 'marketing at the touch of a button', you still want to be sending valuable, timely information to your client list. Sending useful information, rather than random 'marketing' will keep you at the head of the pack.

That got me thinking how cool it would be to see just how SmallBizDream.com may help a real estate agent make larger commissions without a lot of extra busy work.

I started to think about myself as both a rental unit owner and a homeowner and what kind of follow up long term would have kept me feeling endeared to my realtor, and even in a place where I wanted to refer them my friend's vs feeling they were pushy.

I thought about all the cool things I learned over the years as far as maintaining a property and how it can affect resale. I would have been happy to hear from my realtor if it included some aftercare tips on my primary residence, OR my rental properties. It would have been even better if they were timely and topical to the age and type of properly I purchased.

What if 1 month after buying my home I got a nice email suggesting things I can do each month to keep my home in tip top shape?

Things like:

- Check Furnace Filter and replace if needed
- Clean kitchen sink disposal (garburator)
- Clean range hood filters (I know, nobody does this monthly, but imagine how easy it would be if you DID!)
- Inspect your fire extinguishers (or gentle reminder to get a few!)
- I likely wouldn't even mind if I got this each month for 2 or 3 months until it became a habit for me!

Maybe the second month include information on how to do each task, or good things to search on google, or YouTube videos you found to show how easy it is to do them.

What if I got an email Quarterly to share the things I should do quarterly like:

- Test Smoke Detector
- Test Carbon dioxide detectors
- Test your garage door auto reverse function
- Run water and flush toilets in unused bathrooms or sinks
- Check your water softener and add salt if needed.
- Ok how about Bi-annually things like:
- Check water heaters pressure relief valve
- Give your house a good deep cleaning (could also do annually)
- Vacuum your refrigerator coils (this can save considerable energy consumption)

What if they sent me an email timed to the seasons to remind me of things that should be done seasonally?

Spring

- Check for standing water around your house and fix if you find it
- Do a walk around your house looking for siding issues, paint issues, holes in brick, animal or insect infestations, cracks in foundation inside or out.
- If you have air conditioning get it serviced before it gets busy and more expensive to do so closer to the summer.
- Clear dead plants or shrubs
- Make sure no electrical line interference issues
- Inspect your roof for damage on the outside or leaks

from the inside.

- Wash windows and Put your screens up.
- Check and clean gutters if necessary
- Pressure wash away mold or moss on deck and house.
- Service your lawnmower
- Fertilize your lawn
- Dust blinds
- Vacuum curtains
- Uncover Air Conditioners
- Open crawl space vents
- Steam Clean Carpets

Summer

- Check grout and caulking in bathrooms and kitchens repair or re-do as you find issues.
- Clean aerators on faucets
- Check plumbing under each sink to ensure not leaking
- Spray for insects if you need to, summer is when they make the most trouble for your home.
- Clean and repair your deck. Re-stain/re-paint if necessary.
- Clean out any accumulated junk or plant matter in window wells if you have them.
- Check/clean dryer vent and any other vents exhausting to outside
- Vacuum lint from your dryer hose
- Clean out your garage!
- Get your chimney cleaned

Fall

- Flush your hot water heater
- Winterize Air Conditioner
- Annual Heater checkup/cleaning
- Check all caulking on windows and weather stripping is in good shape and replace if it isn't.
- Test sump pump if you have one
- Check driveway for cracks and get them sealed before winter to prevent cracks from spreading
- Get prepared for winter with shovels, salt etc. if you are in a snowy or cold winter area.
- Take your window screens down, label and store them so they are easily put back up in the spring. Get any repair done now while its cheap and nobody is busy
- Do a yard cleanup
- Check outdoor faucets for leaks, then drain and turn off.
- Store any outdoor hoses
- Clean gutters and downspouts.
- Clean, oil, and store garden tools
- Clean and store your patio furniture
- Do a fire drill with the family
- Check attic for leaks, and insulation and pests.
- Cover Air conditioners
- Test snow blower and service if necessary before the rush

Winter

- Regularly clear icicles and ice dams
- Test all the electrical outlets in your home to make sure they are working.
- Test your ground fault interrupt to be sure they work.

- Check the house for any loose screws, or loose fittings
- Check all locks and deadbolts on doors, gates, windows, skylights.
- Clean your showerheads of sediment and limescale.
- Do a deep cleaning on your basement and ensure no mold growing.
- Close any crawlspace vents in your foundation

Okay, so that is just over 60 reasons any home owner would be HAPPY to hear from their real estate agent, OR potential real estate agent!

Other things came to mind as reasons my realtor or a NEW REALTOR I MET, could have followed up in a positive manner to eventually win my business:

- A Christmas card/email
- A birthday card/email
- An anniversary card/email – must stay in contact to make sure still married ;)

A great technique we teach at SmallBizDream.com is the Beer, or Wine or Spirits follow up. This works when you meet them in a social setting and have the opportunity to learn what their favorite drink is.

Once you have learned this, you use a tool like SmallBizDream.com to tag them, AND add them to an email series that will reach out at an obscure time a month or so letting them know you met them at a networking event or barbeque and they said their favorite beverage was beer (or whatever they told you), then you simply ask for a good beer recommendation to take to your friend's house that is also a beer lover.

Of course, your email signature line links to your sales funnel site, and/or offers the ability to join your free home maintenance follow up reminder, or get a free market assessment from you.

But how does all this translate into more commissions?

As I'm sure you're aware, there is a long sales cycle in real estate. The average North American sells their home every 13 years. If this is the case, you probably don't want to follow up for 13 years just to make a sale. You'll go BROKE in the meantime.

What about referrals? Do you think a home buyer or seller may tell their friends about you if you had been the one helping them keep their house in tip top shape? Maybe your tips were timely enough to save them a financial disaster; you think they may think about you a bit more?

Eventually their children or grandchildren also will likely buy homes. Don't you want to be the one they call?

What are you currently doing NOW to ensure they remember you and respect you enough to refer you or call you many years later? Now what if we could monetize it even more?

What if you could team up with the appropriate professionals, and include them in your email follow up. Get them to agree to a 10% back to you for the referral. Make sure you know and trust these people by trying them yourself first. This would sure backfire if you gave a bad referral from Craig's list.

Imagine all the services you could help with and pick up a small margin and a reason to be remembered and loved by your clients.

Annually:

- Carpet Cleaning 2200 square-foot home approx. $362 per Angie's list so if you got 10% of that $36.20
- Gutter Cleaning – average per homeadvisor.com $146 x 10% = $14.60
- Air Conditioner service -average per Angie's list $85 x 10% = $8.50
- Furnace service average per Angie's list $75 x 10% = $7.50

- Exterminator – general pest control per Angie's list $300 x 10% = $30

Total Annual extras easily attainable: $96.80!

Let's say it averages out to $100/year/customer for 13 years, that's $1300 EXTRA commissions earned by being the awesome Real Estate Agent we know you want to be, AND you secure the next sale and referrals.

If you are the average real estate agent who sells 4 to 6 homes per year, say 5 for the sake of math.

5 homes in year one yield you ADDITIONAL 5 x $100 = $500
5 more homes in year 2 = $500 + $500 = $1000
5 in year 3 = $500 + $500 + $500 = $1500
5 in year 4 = $2000
5 in year 5 = $2500
5 in year 6 = $3000
5 in year 7 = $3500
5 in year 8 = $4000
5 in year 9 = $4500
5 in year 10 = $5000
5 in year 11 = $5500
5 in year 11 = $6000
5 in year 12 = $6500
5 in year 13 = $7000

You are now making a residual $7000/year for helping your previous customers.

Now if the averages work out, your first 5 home buyers are ready to re-buy, so you have the big commissions coming, but in the meantime, you have covered your real estate business expenses if you simply had a system to automatically recommend a few choice vendors you form relationships with, and share them with your customers.

If you are the average Real Estate agent making $40,000 or so annually, that is a 17.5% increase in your annual income!

What if you sold 10 homes per year?

You'll get $14,000 in extra commissions for doing a good service for your clients.

I have no way to calculate how many more referrals you would get and additional business just by always being in the top of your previous customers minds in a very helpful and meaningful way!

Would it take some effort? Small Business Dream could help you to automate and semi-automate almost all of it. We have a template you can get with all the things discussed already set up and built in. www.smallbizdream.com/realtor to learn more

It would take some time to research the 5 or 6 vendors you plan to recommend, and some time to write up some email series (as mentioned smallbizdream.com has a bunch of this type of content built-in for realtors!)

You also need to be careful about disclosure laws in your real estate jurisdiction.

What if Small Business Dream could also remind you to call EACH AND EVERY home owner once a year close to their purchase or sale anniversary. Just touch base, say hello, catch up, see if email is still current, see if they are liking your email reminders.

Sales Automation is not always just about getting you new business, it is often equally or more powerful in getting you MORE business from your existing Customers!

Let's look at how you may set up Small Business Dream specifically to use this Home Maintenance reminder concept to give value to even currently low value prospects.

Start with the most important questions that will enable you to know how to follow up with this prospect;

Do they rent or own? Based on their answer, follow up with deeper questions related to specific answers.

You could set up a Step Survey to get the information you need to follow up specifically. This same Step Survey could be used on either a prospect at a networking event, or linked to from your LinkedIn profile, website, or sales funnel.

A Step Survey is a dynamic survey series which, based on the answers given, asks more personalized, targeted questions the further the participant gets. This increase both engagement, and the likelihood they will answer all your survey questions.

One huge survey with many non-relevant questions and answers almost never gets filled in accurately.

Here is how the first survey could look:
Step 1 Survey (make survey called "RentOrOwn")
Do you Rent or Own your home now?

- Rent – On Submit send to "Rent" Survey
- Own – On Submit send to "Own" Survey

You should make your survey to go to a Step 2 survey based upon If they answer rent or own: (make survey called "Rent" with these questions/answers)

If they answered Rent, try this as Step 2 Survey content.

You shared with me you are a renter; please give me a more detail to help me serve you best.

1. How long have you been a renter?
    a. 1yr
    b. 2yr
    c. 5yr
    d. 10yr+

2. What type of home do you rent?

a. Apartment
b. Condo
c. Townhome
d. Single family detached

3. Do you see yourself buying a home in the future?
   a. Yes - On Submit send to "RentBuyYes" Survey
   b. No
   c. Maybe

4. Have you ever owned your own home before?
   a. Yes
   b. No

Based upon the answers given in the Step 2 Survey "Rent" you can drop them off to a Step 3 Survey.

If they answered "Own" (make survey called "RentBuyYes")

You said on our Renting survey you were considering buying a place in the future. Please help me understand your needs better so I can provide the best service to you.

How many years before you plan to buy?

Less than 1 year

1 to 2 years

2 to 5 years

More than 5 years from now.

No plan to buy now.

What do you want to buy?

Apartment

Condo

Townhome

Single family detached

What price range are you thinking of?

Under $100,000
$100,000 to $250,000
$250,000 to $500,000
$500,000 to $750,000
$750,000 to $2 Million
$2 Million to $5 Million

If they say on Step 1 Survey "RentOrOwn" they "Own" their place, your Step 2 Survey could be:

Great! You are a homeowner, please share a few more details so I can follow up with you in a meaningful manner.

How old is your home?
Under 2 years
2 to 5 years
5 to 10 years
10 to 15 years
15 to 20 years
20 years +
When did you buy your home?
Less than 1 year ago
1 to 2 years ago
2 to 5 years ago
5 to 10 years ago
10 to 15 years ago
15 years or longer ago.
What kind of home do you own?
Condo
Townhouse
Single Family Detached

What do think your home is worth in todays market? (Of course, follow up to this is would they like to give you a market assessment for

FREE?)

Under $100,000

$100,000 to $250,000

$250,000 to $500,000

$500,000 to $750,000

$750,000 to $2 Million

$2 Million to $5 Million

No Idea.

How long before you plan to sell your home?

In less than 1 year

In 1 to 2 years

In 2 to 5 years

More than 5 years from now.

No plan to sell now.

Would you like to join our Home Maintenance reminder list?

Yes please

No thank you

What is that?

Would you like to have a ton of email content you could use as a realtor to follow up? Rather than put it into this book, please grab a FREE version of our Realtor template of SmallBizDream.com from SmallBizDream.com/realtor. It's an easy way to stay top of mind with all your clients.

Footnotes:
http://www.artofmanliness.com/2013/10/08/keep-your-house-in-tip-top-shape-an-incredibly-handy-home-maintenance-checklist/
http://www.lowes.com/cd_Home+Maintenance+Schedule+and+Checklist_1297357358_
http://www.angieslist.com/articles/what-are-average-carpet-cleaning-prices.htm
http://www.homeadvisor.com/cost/cleaning-services/clean-gutters-and-downspouts/
http://www.angieslist.com/videos/video-5-things-know-about-ac-

maintenance.htm

http://www.angieslist.com/articles/how-often-should-you-have-furnace-inspection.htm

CREATING A BUYING PERSONA TO GUIDE YOUR MARKETING EFFORTS

Businesses worldwide are constantly upgrading their strategies to maximize their ROI (Return On Investment) in their marketing efforts. Some notable examples include email, social media marketing, content marketing, CRM integration, and creating a detailed buyer persona specific to a given industry.

The buyer persona epitomizes their constant efforts to stay relevant with their customers. The shift from generalized, stereotypical advertising to individualized customer engagement is one the most remarkable steps in the history of trade and industry and has changed the way companies and business establishments market themselves to world.

Buyer Persona: What it is, and what it's Not!

Buyer persona is coined from the word 'persona', often associated with psychology When applied to business, it means an ideal customer with the most desirable traits suitable for marketing.

This 'model customer' serves as the basis for the company's design, production, and marketing efforts from which they can generate income. Different industries can have several buyer personas, each having unique, individual characteristics that mirror their real-life equivalents.

However, there are some common misconceptions about the buyer persona, one of which is the old practice of stereotyping customers popular among traditional businesses. They would try to fit every customer into a certain category and make sweeping generalizations about their customers based on assumptions and mere speculation.

The fundamental difference between a buyer persona and a stereotype is the depth of insight into the customer's own circumstances – his work, lifestyle, education, hobbies, expertise, expectations, buying standards, etc. A stereotype barely scratches the surface and provides an incomplete picture of your target market while a buyer persona goes deeper by creating a life-like representation of your ideal customers based on facts and relevant data.

The Buyer Persona's Role in Business

The company's marketing efforts gravitate on the customer's ever-changing needs personified by the buyer persona. Without a proper understanding of their customers, all their efforts from production to marketing, to sales conversion would be in jeopardy.

A well-researched buyer persona not only safeguards their business interests but it also guides them on what product or service – with its many variants and slight nuances – to provide their customers and how they can successfully market them across different channels.

How a Buyer Persona is Born

The first step in creating an all-inclusive buyer persona is to collect as much information as possible about previous and current customers. Some of the ways to do this are to conduct surveys and interviews from a wide range of potential customers regarding their opinions on certain products or services. Sources include demographic information of a particular area, CRM data, email marketing tools, social media and Google Analytics. These data points will serve as the building blocks for your buyer persona's 'DNA'.

The process can take some time and effort before one can make an accurate representation of an ideal customer. In some instances, it is necessary to create two or more data points for each type of customer and/or customer preference. Finally, the company breathes life to the buyer persona by giving it a personalized name and image.

What to Include in a Buyer Persona

During the process of its creation, business firms compile information from various sources and try to make a unified picture of their imaginary customer. The following information will help you determine what your buyer persona would be:

Demographic information
Age bracket
Gender
Country/Nationality
Language
Personal information
Educational attainment
Profession/Occupation
Civil Status
Income Level
Customer information
Buying History
Buying Motivation
Buying Preference
Average Spending
Specific Skills and Interests

There are plenty of ways you can extract the given information about your leads. Statistical information about people in a certain area can be easily obtained from government sources. Acquiring personal and customer information at the lowest level may take some time because it involves actual conversation with people and encouraging them to participate in a survey but is very valuable. Properly implementing a CRM like Small Business Dream can assist greatly in getting this type of information to flow up from the sales floor or sales team.

However, digital workarounds have made this job a lot easier. Social networking sites like Facebook, Google and Twitter are treasure trove when it comes to personal information, skills, and interests about your leads and customers. A lot of companies have been using social media to collect information about their 'fans' and 'followers' as part of their marketing strategy.

If your company doesn't have a Facebook or Twitter account, consider social media marketing as a way of gathering relevant information about your target market. You might still need to engage them personally to fill in the gaps, particularly with sensitive information like their income level, net worth, etc.

When it comes to customer information of previous and current customers, nothing comes close to CRM customer data. Depending on the type of CRM service, businesses can track down their customer's buying habits, monitor existing trends, and predict customer behavior.

With CRM, businesses stay up-to-date with its constant supply of data from day to day transactions with current customers. That is why successful businesses turn to their CRM when creating buyer personas to zero in on their target market and maximize their income potential.

Look for the right CRM service to guide you. Some consulting agencies offer CRM services to help you with the process of creating a realistic, data-inspired buyer persona. Small Business Dream offers a suite of tools in customer acquisition, sales funnel, sales, marketing and email automation for small business owners like you.

HOW A SALON USED CUSTOMER RELATIONSHIP MANAGEMENT TO BOOST SALES

Once upon a time in a city far, far away, there was a little hair salon that decided to do the unthinkable. The hair salon owner decided to try and actually follow up with their hair salon clients to check in, not only on customer satisfaction with the hair stylist, but also to increase their sales frequency and profit.

Here is the surprisingly simple way the hair salon owner did it. First, the salon owner made sure to give every customer a client number and a simple loyalty card for the Hair Salon. This started as a stamp type loyalty card, very simple. It had a place to write by hand, the clients name, and their ID number on the card.

Once the customer visited the hair studio 10 times, they were entitled to one of many free services, which included a hair color, hair protein treatment, a hair wash dry and set, a bottle of shampoo, or a color root touch up.

In order to prepare the customer card, the little hair salon owner had customers fill in a simple survey pertinent to a hair salon, including the customer's phone number, email address and hair styling preferences, and known allergies. They also offered all new hair salon clients the chance to opt-in to their weekly hair styling newsletter, and if they did, they would be placed in a draw for a free monthly $50 gift card for the salon OR a local restaurant. Notice they didn't just say for the salon? This is an important point to getting engagement in a Newsletter. If the "reward" is so focused on your own business, people feel like it is just a big sales pitch vs. an actual prize.

Next, the hair salon owner was very progressive and set up some simple sales and marketing automation software (yes, you guessed it, Small Business Dream) in order to follow up with the customers over the next few months.

As customers have enough cards to carry around, the hair salon owner decided to keep the loyalty cards at the front desk for the customer so they never needed to remember it, they simply needed to give their name.

Every time a customer came in to the hair salon, the receptionist or a stylist found their card and confirmed their number.

After the client was done with their haircut or hair service they came for, the hair stylist pulled up their information in Small Business Dream, filled in what hair services the customer had done in the notes field, as well as any other pertinent details that would allow them to better service this customer the next time they came in to the hair salon, and reset their automated email follow up campaign. (email autoresponder)

The email campaign was a big key to the increase in sales in the hair salon. It was structured in the following way.

The day after the hair appointment, the hair salon sent an email from the hair salon owner checking in on the previous days service and asking for feedback if anything was wrong and how the hair stylist performed. This surprised the salon as the owner got both GOOD and BAD feedback about the hair stylists they employed. This allowed them to rectify errors and retain good customers even in the event of a mishap.

Check out the video at twt.bz/salon

Two weeks after the hair appointment, they sent an email letting the customer know they could pop in for a professional wash, dry, and hair set for just $30, a way to get the hair salon look at a fraction of the cost for a special occasion

Four weeks after the appointment, they sent an email asking if it might be about time to come and get a haircut again.

They were stunned by how many responses this email got, and very positive ones, actually thanking the hair salon owner for the reminder stating the customer often forgot to book, and this email reminded them to get it done and it was simple, as they just replied by email, to book the time they wanted. This system made it easy for the customer to book a hair styling appointment.

Now the cool part of this was, this took the average rebooking time from 7 to 8 weeks, to averaging 6 weeks, which meant a MASSIVE increase in annual sales.

Here's the math (yuck) on how this increased sales frequency generated by the sales and marketing automation software (smallbizdream.com) affected the hair salons sales and profitability

(Yes!);

Let's say your average hair salon sale is $65 and your customers come in every 8 weeks.

This means your hair salon customers comes to see you about 52/8 = 6.5 times per year. Your average annual sales from your hair salon's clients are 6.5 x $65 = $422.50. If you got them back an average of 1 time each 6 weeks instead, it would be 52/6 = 8.67 times.

Your average annual sales form a client then would be 8.67 x $65 = $563.33.

That is $140.83 additional hair salon revenue per client. This is a WHOPPING 33% increase in Annual Sales!!!! What if you only had 500 hair salon clients? $70,415 extra sales annually What if you had 1000?

$140,830!!

At 6 weeks, an email went out suggesting it was time to re-book a haircut as they were likely getting pretty shaggy.

Then at 8 weeks, an apology email went out, YEP, that's right, they apologized for not doing a good enough job to have the client come back to the hair salon and they offered at 10% discount with the apology email if the customer rebooked within 3 days.

At 12 weeks, an extension of the apology re-offering the 10% off went out, and tossing in a free bottle of shampoo, or free protein treatment if they booked again in the next 3 days.

This wasn't as random as it sounds, they knew their average time of rebook was 7 weeks, so at 8 weeks it was likely frustrated customer, or a super cheap one that would wait 10 or 12 weeks to come back. By offering the 10% they made the unhappy client feel cared for, and often coaxed the cheaper customer to come again to chase the discount. This again drove annual sales up dramatically by increasing customer frequency.

Once the hair salon had collected its customer database

including email address, it also started to implement a Web Special page on its hair salon website that it email blasted out each 2 weeks as part of their bi-weekly newsletter.

The web specials page contained super hair salon amazing deals, sometimes as much as 50% off, but only for specific hair stylists and time slots. They used it to fill their empty seats, this decreased dramatically their sales vacancy and once again increased their hair salon profits.

If the hair salon ever got in a real bind with hair stylists having empty seats, they did an instant blast to everybody offering a great hair salon service deal on a super short time frame to fill that spot. It may have been a haircut, or a hair color, or even a hair straightening, it just depended on what the hair salon could handle in the time available.

The results were out of this world. The Hair Stylist's empty seat time vanished. Stylists made more money in tips. The hair salon owner made more money as a hair salon. Other hair stylists started to want to work there as they heard how busy the hair salon always was.

Another benefit the hair salon found as it implemented its simple CRM sales and marketing automation software to track and follow up with its customers, was the ability to track Customer Preferences to increase customer satisfaction.

One of the final things the hair salon owner put in place was a reminder phone call, text (SMS), Facebook message, or any other method of communication the customer had indicated they preferred for all appointments coming up the next day. Small Business Dream made this easy for the hair stylists to do, so they weren't as likely to try to skip it!

This simple action decreased no-shows to the hair salon significantly, and made the customer feel extremely cared for.

In today's online world, the likes of Yelp and others are making it more and more important to have at least a simple web presence for review and referral sites to link to. By having your own hair salon website, all the ranking sites for Hair Salons will send traffic to your site where you control the narrative, vs. scraping information they can find publicly available about your hair salon.

As a result of this and the web-specials concept, the hair salon put together a simple website (smallbizdream.com also allows you to build a simple website for this purpose) and even started to use their new found cash flow to do super targeted advertising on Facebook, Twitter and Google AdWords.

This traffic simply was directed to the hair salon's website which had the ability to sign up to the newsletter for the possibility of winning that $50 gift certificate. This drove engagements, and the ability for the email follow up series to be employed to convert this look and see traffic to an actual customer.

The final thing the hair salon owner did was implement a referral program. They simply offered anybody who had their friend signup to the hair salon newsletter would earn one draw per person they referred into the draw for a $100 gift certificate at the hair salon (drawn monthly). This turned happy clients into referring advocates or fans! It grew their list dramatically, which converted to new hair salon customers over time.

Lets re-cap the important bits that led to this astounding sales growth:

1. A system with the ability to make a simple website and web specials page
2. The ability to have data collected and used for an email blast like web specials or a weekly newsletter.
3. The ability to collect data on prospects generated by Facebook and Google, and follow up with them automatically over time with a timed series of emails to convert them to a client.
4. The ability to make a calling list of all appointments the next day easily and take notes as you make the calls.

The best part is, we have a template of the hair salon system readily available in Small Business Dream, so you simply need to make minor tweaks to the content and you should be up and running in a very short time reaping the rewards of good sales automation.

HOW MARKET AUTOMATION CAN HELP SMALL BUSINESS

Marketing automation is at the core of almost every online business today, and should also be a key strategy in more traditional businesses as well.

As a cost-effective way to reach out potential customers, this strategy has proved time and again that anyone – with sufficient knowledge, tools, and skill sets – can have a fair chance to compete with other businesses worldwide.

However, even the most innovative online strategy has a downside. For years, marketing automation has become the subject of misuse among online marketers who pitched automation as a way of turning businesses into online 'cash machines' without ever spending time and effort with potential customers. It made marketing automation synonymous to spamming.

Faced with more competition, stringent rules regarding customer engagement, and increased customer awareness, online marketers are back to the drawing board on how they could use automation to deliver the same results back in its heyday, or even better.

Why a Change of Strategy is Necessary.

When marketing automation was at its peak, many believed as long as you were able to make tons of content and send a relentless barrage of emails to practically any person on earth that has an email address, sooner or later people would respond to your call and generate income for your business.

The idea comes from the analogy of shooting as many arrows as you can, hoping one or two will eventually land on their target out of mere chance (known as the 'spray and pray' method). Although some businesses use this method effectively, it usually comes at a price.

For one thing, marketers who rely heavily on conventional marketing automation are putting their businesses at risk by sending unsolicited emails to people whose contact information were sourced from a third-party data supplier. This method obviously won't work, since most emails have already built defenses against spamming.

For Canadian Small Business Owners, the CAN-SPAM Act will also make these marketers think twice about ever using this method again. The fines for spamming electronically in ANY way are out of this world!

Aside from bordering unlawful marketing practices, it tends to yield diminishing returns over time as contacts starts falling off and fewer people become available to them. It usually guarantees a one-time success with little or no regard for ongoing customer relationship and repeat purchases.

Staying relevant with the customers is almost impossible to attain with conventional marketing automation. Usually, what happens is companies will send all the content they have on a particular niche to people on their massive lists, hoping to strike a chord with just one or two articles sent to them in rapid succession. It's essentially a 'hit-or-miss' strategy.

As customer engagement comes close to non-existent, they would eventually lose their ship, and no amount of automation can save it from sinking to the bottom. The question now is whether full marketing automation can still be a viable option to speed up the process and boost sales despite its potential shortcomings in customer engagement.

A Step Towards Permission Marketing

Permission marketing was coined by marketing expert Seth Godin to denote marketing strategies that rely on customer feedback, i.e., permission, to initiate ongoing customer relationship and interaction which allows them to receive updates and follow-ups on demand.

Unlike traditional outbound marketing, which he appropriately calls 'interruption marketing', permission marketing spares people the trouble of going through the ordeal of being constantly bombarded with marketing pitches. It gives them more freedom and control over the situation and encourages them to either share more about their interests and other key information about themselves, or turn into buying customers.

Others tend to view permission marketing as the antithesis of marketing automation because it's more involved and requires frequent human interaction. The fact is, permission marketing needs a starting point, and that involves automation. This is the sweet spot of digital marketing. Sign-up forms via landing pages, which may also include opt-in to newsletters or social media posts, are just a few classic examples on how to initiate permission marketing.

Still others believe permission marketing is a little too slow compared to marketing automation aside from the fact it gives too much freedom to potential customers to take action whenever they want to. They aim for quick, albeit short-lived gains, instead of nurturing previous and current customers for long-term, sustainable income.

In the final analysis, those who relied on one-time customer engagements end up losing more money looking for new prospects while those who took their time watering and growing their customer base could increase revenue exponentially through updates, follow-ups, customer referrals, crossing-selling, up-selling, and repeat purchases.

The Smart Way to Automate

Marketing automation platforms can only do so well when it comes to tasks lending themselves well to automation. Some aspects of marketing are best performed through human interaction which cannot be copied or supplanted by automated means.

Keep these in mind when using marketing automation to attract and maintain customers for your business. We suggest you consider a combination of fully automated, and semi-automated sales and marketing automation.

You should open multiple channels to collect customer information. Inbound marketing has proven its effectiveness over outbound marketing by emphasizing customer awareness. Utilizing multiple channels of customer engagement maximizes your chances of getting in touch with them. This could include setting up things like a blog, website, landing page, and even new social media accounts, to name a few. Your marketing automation platform can be seamlessly integrated to all these channels to collect, store, and analyze customer information for you after joining your mailing list or subscribing to your free newsletter.

Marketing automation shines best at this stage of customer engagement and I would like to now share a few tips to make it EVEN better with micro-targeting and semi-automation.

Make sure anytime you are collecting data from a website you do it with a simple survey, or if your questions are more complicated, use a proper squeeze survey. A squeeze survey simply means you do not ask 20 questions on one survey, but rather ask for more information in a secondary survey acknowledging utilization questions answered in the first survey.

For example, let's say you are a realtor. You sell residential and commercial real estate. If you simply asked in your first survey what they were interested in, AFTER collecting their data, you could take them to a secondary survey stating, "you said you were interested in commercial real estate, so we had a few follow-up questions to assist us in helping you the best.

You can then go through as many steps of the survey you see fit with this technique. With good CRM like Small Business Dream, each answer to a question could be categorizing the client, adding them to email or social media follow up series, taking them OUT of other series no longer relevant due to the new information obtained.

This is Micro Targeting at its finest. They gave up information to you, and you sent out Commercial Real Estate regarding 10 story or less apartment rental buildings under $10 million information AUTOMATICALLY but highly focused!

Now, semi-automation has become critical in today's marketplace. Rather than send fully automated generic information to everybody, especially in the social media communications area, have a system like Small Business Dream that allows you to create a series of communications to go out by SMS or FB Messenger, or even email. The bulk of information is set and automated, but you customize a sentence or two before sending.

The increases engagements when the communication makes a comment about the awesome picture of the pink Volkswagen beetle on their profile before getting into your message. They don't feel automated!

The key to great sales automation and semi-automation is being UNDETECTED!

Dissect your sales pipeline to see which approach works best in every stage. In case you haven't noticed this has been alluded to previously. The first stage, which involves data collection and storage, is best accomplished with marketing automation and semi-automation. Following up, which is the next stage, involves a combination of both permission marketing and marketing automation, semi-automation, and micro targeting.

When trying to learn more about your leads, you can revert back to automation to, once again, collect relevant information about them by sending out a short survey offering a gift certificate to all who take the time to answer and analyze whether or not they could be qualified as potential customers for a particular product or service you offer. The marketing team would then assign the lead scores, start with the sales process, and close the deal.

Use email segmentation (micro targeting) and the buyer persona to guide your marketing efforts. These marketing strategies allow you to narrow down your target audience and zero in on them with pinpoint accuracy. Unfortunately, it takes time and effort to create relevant content based on different segments and customer behavior but it's worth it.

The easiest way to fail in any kind of marketing strategy is to use the same cut-and-dried content across all contacts and send them out at a robotic pace, one email after another.

You need to customize your content according to the different segments in your email list and provide an option for a follow-up or additional information about the topic.

Choose a marketing automation platform that works for you, of course we are biased to Small Business Dream at smallbizdream.com.

A good marketing automation AND semi-automation platform often comes at a price. However, most companies offer different versions of their product ranging from the most basic ones at no cost, to premium offerings with a complete suite of tools at aa hundred thousand, or even tens of thousands of dollars per month depending on your needs and company size.

If you're a startup company, you may want to use the free version first to get acquainted with the ins and outs of marketing automation and get the feel of how you can integrate permission marketing along with other tools available for you in the marketing app suite. Small Business Dream has a free forever version that allows you to do 2000 communications per month at smallbizdream.com

Marketing automation can still be as powerful as any marketing strategy if you can put other elements into the mix such as permission marketing to interact with your potential customers and gain sufficient data about your target market.

PART II: SOCIAL MEDIA

HOW TO BEAT YOUR COMPETITION USING SOCIAL MEDIA

Social media is still one of the most misunderstood marketing tools for small business. If you're not using it, you're missing out on a valuable opportunity to drive customers to your website and ultimately make a purchase.

According to a recent LinkedIn study, a whopping 81% of businesses use social media to drive growth while an additional 9% intend to use social media in the future. If your online presence isn't up to par, you may think you missed out, social media is too crowded, but it's still a vital way for businesses to reach their customers, if done correctly.

Unfortunately, most businesses don't understand how to use it to connect with their customers and drive the results they want.

Consumers now are savvier than ever before and do their research before making a purchasing decision and that includes searching a businesses' social media presence. In today's competitive world, small businesses need to have a solid online presence if they expect to be successful. A lot of people won't trust or do business with a company that doesn't have an online presence. If they don't see a strong following on any of the channels it might mean they choose somebody with more social proof. Customers are also more likely to take their grievances out online and it's crucial for businesses to respond to customer inquiries and reviews.

You shouldn't just be reactive online. Social media is cheaper than doing a national advertisement campaign on television and can reach the same amount of people. Grab people's attention with creative social media content.

The age of your customers will also determine how you communicate with them online. Millennials are more skeptical and typically want to know who the owner of a business is more so than older customers.

Part of the problem with social media is that small business have a hard time tracking return on investment. It can especially be hard to track organic social media and for a small business on a tight budget, it is usually the first thing to go. Google Analytics is free and can certainly help, but it does take some time to learn. We highly suggest you learn and utilize this to help know the effectiveness of your Social Media work.

However, for those who invest consistently in social media, most agree there is a payoff within the first two years and a significant payoff in five years. A small caveat here. It's important you don't try to compete with the big companies, especially online. They have people, sometimes entire departments, dedicated entirely to social media and their online presence. You must think how you can carve your own space out online. Perhaps it's coming up with a unique and exciting campaign, maybe it's dominating a local area. Our vote is always to go after a local area and blanket it. It is far cheaper than you would think.

For the last couple years, Facebook and other social media platforms have been pushing people to paid advertising instead of organic content. Paid social media has enormous upside and is cost effective compared to other forms of advertising. Here's the thing, no amount of paid social media is going to turn bad creative into good content. For the most part, it isn't sustainable for small businesses on a tight budget.

However organic content is still incredibly powerful and when used correctly, it can be incredibly effective. Organic content is the long-game plan of your brand.

For example, if you use hashtags properly, you can easily be discovered over time. Whether you're a local restaurant or coffee shop, if you keep using relevant hashtags then you'll be a part of the conversation which is the first step to getting sales.

If you're a small business you want to focus your time, money and effort on creating lots of great content. The amount of money you spend on social media depends on your industry and marketing goals.

The biggest thing businesses don't understand is quality content is extremely important to market to anyone under the age of 40. Anyone in that demographic usually discovers a business for the first time with a Google search or though their content on social media. If you're not focused on quality content you put out on the most important social platforms, you're going to become irrelevant. That's why organic reach is so important because the impressions you get when someone comes directly to your page create a more qualified lead and a potentially more valuable customer.

There are plenty of platforms out there for you to choose from that will help you grow your audience, from Facebook, LinkedIn, Instagram to Twitter. You should decide what is right for you and your small business.

While the supply and demand for paid advertisement becomes more competitive and saturated there is a greater opening for brands to make headway organically.

HOW ALL THE SOCIAL MEDIA EXPERTS GOT IT WRONG

We all know email is a powerful tool to follow up with your prospects and customers but social media can be equally as powerful if you use it correctly. The problem is that most so-called experts have it dead wrong! They think it's about posting as frequently as possible when in fact, it's about having a clear, concise message and engaging people through proper follow up.

Now let's be clear, as with all types of messages: DON'T SPAM people! What's the difference between proper messaging and spamming?

The key is to provide value and message them about something they are actually interested in! Don't talk about yourself like some egotistical fool! Engage them with information that is relevant and important to them or their business and engage with them in a two-way dialogue.

How do you do that?

You want your follow up to be semi-automated so you set up a series with a very specific idea of what you intend to say over time and then when your CRM like Small Business Dream (smallbizdream.com) brings up that communication to be sent, you simply add a line that is completely custom and recognizably so by the recipient. A comment on a life or business event you saw on their social media, or a picture or video you saw on their social media or website. Then you copy and paste the entire custom message into your Facebook messenger,

LinkedIn messenger, Line, WhatsApp, WeChat etc. and you send it.

It is the 80/20 rule. 80% of your communications must create BENEFIT to the recipient, 20% leading to benefit to you.

I talked to someone who was using social media as part of her sales funnel. She was posting messages in Facebook groups but she wasn't individually messaging them and she wasn't following up with them. When you use any sort of sales message you need to follow up, politely but firmly.

You're not studying how Facebook works anymore. Only about two percent of people are seeing what you post and it's about to go to one percent! Two percent of all your Facebook group people, unless they specifically go to your Facebook group and look at what's there, won't see your message. Facebook has strictly become a pay-to-play network! Most of your connections won't see what you've written on your news feed. The problem is if you're relying on groups and posts for all your communications, you're missing out on a lot.

Isn't it interesting social networking has made a bunch of things easier, but has made us so lazy we don't follow up. We think because they joined our Facebook group, anything we post there, they're seeing and they'll take action.

The good news is that it's still relatively inexpensive to boost a post. It's definitely worth it to spend a couple bucks on each post to make sure people are seeing it. The added benefit of boosting a post is that you also increase the organic reach. They piggyback off each other. If I boost a post for seven bucks I get over a 500-organic reach. Not bad for the price of a Triple Venti Mocha! Of course the cost will likely go up as Facebook has practically a monopoly on social media advertisement.

If you're smart, you'll use a customer management tool that actually reminds you to restart the conversation when you've not been in contact for a while. SmallBizDream.com can do that. Once you come to the realization of how important that is, you'll be swatting away the customers!

Everybody out there is all excited about social media, but few figure out if you engage someone on Facebook messenger, you must follow up just as much as you would on the telephone or by email.

With messaging, everything should be a series to get them connected over time. Yes, when we were talking to someone by direct message on LinkedIn or direct message on Instagram or Snapchat or anything, everybody is sending one message and that's it! They give up or worst yet, just plain forget!

As a small business owner, I know you're busy and you have a lot of things on your plate. That's why you need a system that does all your thinking and legwork for you. A sales automation CRM tool that helps reinitiate conversations and says: 'hey, you need to talk to this prospect again! It has been six days… and here is a reminder for you on what you need to say to reengage him!'

If you follow these rules and strategies, you'll have more clients than you'll know what to do with and you'll need help managing all the leads you get.

WHAT IS WRONG WITH TWITTER

Twitter? Really? TWITTER?

We considered long and hard, and argued late into the night with our editorial team on whether to include this Twitter information in the "Small Business Bible", due to Twitter's seemingly uncertain future.

We finally decided there were enough good points related to social media marketing in general it should be included. We hope

Twitter will make a comeback, but it may have to limit is developer access to force it to be LESS automated for spam and more human driven once again.

That said, we hope you enjoy our Twitter Rant!

Check out the video at twt.bz/twitter

We've all heard Twitter being likened to a cocktail party, in which you can mill about and join in on any digital conversation you feel is interesting, and it might have started out that way.

But now it seems Twitter has turned into a cocktail party in a football stadium, during the Super Bowl game.

Here's how I see Twitter working if you follow most of the Twitter gurus, Twitter e-book publishers, and self-professed twitter list building experts. Let's follow through on that cocktail party concept, and assume you're there for the purpose of finding a date, and eventually a girlfriend/ boyfriend, leading to a husband or wife.

The intent seems to have become to say "Hi" to everybody at the party as fast as possible (loosely translated, this equates to randomly follow all of them), in as loud a voice as possible (meaning, use some automated tool to follow them), and try to get a first date with everyone you said "Hi" to within 5 minutes (or get them to follow you back).

Is it me, or does this seem delusional?

You know nothing about the people you said Hi to (or followed), nothing about what they are talking about, or what they do, or what their interests are, nothing about whether or not you have anything in common.

Do you have a huge list of people you know nothing about? **B**ut you still expect them to agree to your first date request? Except you haven't taken the time or the actions that could actually EARN you that first date.

You didn't listen to what they are talking about (actually read what THEY post), you didn't show any interest in them by being interested in anything they said ("Like" something they post), and you didn't brag about how cool you thought they were and how much you have in com-mon by telling others about them! ("re-tweeting a post or giving them a "Mention")

You then show your impatience by waiting only a day or two, with no further communication from you to them before you ex-communicate them for not accepting your date offer! ("un-follow").

Then you brag about your conquests by advertising to the world how many first dates you have had! (I grew by 595 "followers" today) And of course you keep secret how many never called you back. ("un-followed" you) As long as you go on enough first dates, you will continue to grow your ever so valuable list of like-minded folks.

It's noisy, misdirected, misunderstood and even rude. However even though you have such a misguided approach, you manage to find a few to AGREE to have that first date (or they "followed" you back).

Of course, even though you don't even know if you like or are interested in them, and they likely have no idea about you as you are both likely following the same misguided technique, you have your robot secretary (or auto reply tool) show up for you ("direct message") as you are far too busy with your HUGE list of unqualified date prospects to show up in person to explore the possibilities with the one who said they are interested!

If the most common thing to happen, which is your robot secretary (or "direct message") shows up to find out that they also sent their robot secretary (auto reply to "direct message") vs. showing up in per- son, doesn't happen, there are two ways this seems to go, and the first is almost laughable.

Your robot secretary (or your "direct message") sits down, but rather than give a compliment, or engage in a meaningful two sided conversation to get to know you, you quickly tell your date (or your "follower") they have not connected to you the right way to create the most favorable first impression, and you suggest they re-schedule to a different venue, which you conveniently give them the address to (you telling them to 'follow you on Facebook or Instagram, or join your newsletter by the link you've so graciously included, etc.)

Why wouldn't you just engage with them in the medium they FOUND you on FIRST? Warm them up to you, then suggest you have other places they can learn more about you after the first date is over, or in order to agree to that first date. Twitter recently took the 140-character limit off the Direct Message feature, for goodness sake.

The second way we are taught to teach our robot secretaries is even more damaging if that is possible.

Your robot secretary sits down at the date, and gives a pre-recorded generic message that doesn't acknowledge you even read your potential date's profile, or you learned anything about them, vomiting your information all over them being convinced they (as a non-curated follower) are totally into you!

Let's say you fooled your date, they didn't realize it wasn't you, or they knew it wasn't but actually their intention for meeting you was not to care what you say, but try to force you to hear what they had to say, so they agreed to a second date.

The better robot secretaries will help this. They will automatically follow up with some equally random, off-putting self-promotion a few days later. This usually guarantees your date will stop returning your calls (or not read, like, reply, or retweet), or worse yet,

EX-COMMUNICATE YOU (or "un-follow" you). Either way, you're not getting a second date.

Welcome to Twitter. Everybody talking at each other, instead of with and to each other.

Now the idea is to get your first dates to turn into second dates, and second to third, to boyfriend/girlfriend, to marriage.

Let's consider marriage to be the sale.

This to me is Twitter done WRONG! How do we do Twitter the RIGHT way? Read on and find out how to use Twitter and other social media platforms!

DOING IT RIGHT: INTEGRATING SOCIAL MEDIA WITH EMAIL MARKETING

Every time we talk of online marketing, there are two major strategies that will always come up in people's minds: email marketing and social media marketing. This is for good reason.

First of all, email marketing has been around for nearly three decades since it was first used in the 90s as a cost-effective, direct response method to generate massive leads. It still does today.

Around 2000, saw the birth of social networking sites like MySpace and LinkedIn. And just as social networking sites started to gain traction, guess what? Social media marketing came around. It was an instant success, and for a time many companies began using it to promote their brands.

But now things have changed, the online space has become extremely competitive, and we don't see them being used by online marketers the way they used to. They know their previous tactics won't work anymore and so they started rethinking their strategies just to keep their leads rolling in. Why is this so?

Issues with Social Media Marketing

The problem with most online marketers today is they took something extremely good and useful, and turned it into a mindless lead generating tool with no creativity, no real intention of creating meaningful connections or establishing good relationships. They took "the old-school" method of advertisement and simply moved it online. Most of the bad rap social marketing got into is the so-called 'pay-to-play' tactics used to create a superficial and artificial 'likes' or 'followers' with little or no interaction whatsoever. This obviously doesn't work with today's consumers.

However, there are some social media marketers who use legitimate practices to get results, but it takes time and effort (try responding to all the comments to your posts or tweets and you'll get the idea). Aside from that, it also takes talent and creativity just to get people to even 'like' or 'follow' your post in social media. There are few social media marketers who are really good at this.

Another issue with social media marketing is you're piggybacking on somebody else's platform. If for whatever reason the social networking site decides to take down your social media account, goes under, or loses popularity, you'll lose all your connections and you'll have to start over from scratch. Like they used to say, 'own the racecourse, not the racehorse', don't go all out on something you have no control over.

Why People Still Do Email Marketing Today

When social media marketing started to take a large portion of users from just a million users to 1.7 billion worldwide, many believed email marketing is done or it's already dead. The fact is, it is very much alive and it is still the number one marketing tool used by companies to convert their leads and drive sales.

Take a look at what research tells us about email marketing compared to social media marketing:

•77% of consumers are more likely to respond to promotional messages in their emails than their social media accounts;

• 66% of consumers purchased their products because of promotional messages and follow-ups from emails.

• 44% of promotional emails reach the intended consumer as opposed to 4% in Facebook.

• 58% of people who go online check their emails FIRST, followed by search portal (20%), Facebook (11%), news site (5%), company website (3%), and others (3%).

Using Two Different Tools to Achieve ONE Goal

It should be clear to us why email marketing is still the online marketer's best friend when it comes to lead generation and conversion. However, if you're into social media marketing already, there's no point throwing away the baby with the bathwater. Social media does have its own place in your marketing strategies

Think of social media marketing and email marketing as two different tools. If you want to build a house, you need a hammer and a saw to do the job. These two building implements were made with a specific purpose in mind. But they can be used to achieve ONE goal – build a house. Same is true with social media marketing and email marketing. The problem starts when people use the WRONG tools for the WRONG purpose or the RIGHT tools for the WRONG purpose.

Online marketers need to realize people use social media for mass SHARING and email for COMMUNICATING. The bottom line– use the social media to share a very interesting piece of information, but use your email marketing to diligently follow up those people who liked, shared, or followed, your post/tweet. Here are 7 basic tips you can do to accomplish this task:

1. Spend some time working on your social media account's overall appearance, particularly the cover photo, in fact if you are using it for business, make sure you get a professional headshot done.
2. Create a group exclusively for like-minded people who share the same interests and let people join in.

3. Make your posts/tweets as 'catchy', relevant, and timely as possible but remember the 80/20 rule: 80% for benefit of your audience, 20% on your company/product etc.
4. Facebook users can use 'call-to-action' (CTA) buttons to encourage other users to click the link to their landing pages or sign up to their email list.
5. Twitter users can use Twitter cards to view photos, summaries of links/landing pages, or allow followers to download free app or content without leaving the site.
6. Export your 'friends' or 'followers' email accounts for your email marketing campaigns and follow-ups.
7. Design a landing page or a website for your leads. This will be used to extract more information from them and help you fine tune your email marketing strategy. The Small Business Dream Survey function works GREAT for this!

If you're still struggling with your conversion rates with your social media or email marketing efforts, you're definitely not alone. It could be you're not using the tools the way they should be, like following-up with your leads or doing things at random with no sense of purpose or direction.

COLD OUTREACH SHOULD BE PART OF YOUR MARKETING

Cold outreach should be part of your marketing efforts. If you're not, then I can almost guarantee you're not growing your business, and perhaps it's even shrinking. If you're getting by just on referrals or networking opportunities, great, but without a consistent outbound marketing effort, you won't be able to significantly grow your business.

You need to expand your pipeline through a systematic approach of reaching out to potential customers. Cold outreach isn't hard, yet it continues to be a very underutilized tactic. The reason is simple. It's very painful to risk rejection from your prospective customer. Not even the best sales people like cold outreach.

Recently, at Small Business Dream, we decided to try an experiment on LinkedIn doing cold messaging to contacts and potential buyers for our Sales, Marketing, and Email Automation app. We thought what better way to test the capability of SmallBizDream.com CRM then to do a real live demo.

Why LinkedIn?

We chose LinkedIn because it's a fantastic tool to laser target the type of people you want as customers, in our case, business consultants. There has been some criticism about LinkedIn that engagement is extremely low. Studies have shown most people only log on two or three times a month. We found by using SmallBizDream.com to control our LinkedIn outreach and follow up, we got much higher engagement than normal as WE were reminded to pick up text conversations that had stagnated.

Also, since Microsoft bought LinkedIn and gave it a much-needed Facelift, we predict LinkedIn will be a bigger tool for businesses in the future.

Even if Microsoft's gamble doesn't pay off, most people set LinkedIn private messages to go directly to their email, so we weren't too concerned about engagement level. For example, if we send them a message on LinkedIn then it most likely would wind up in their inbox. Maybe even better. In the United States, you can buy email lists, but in Canada it's illegal so it's a good way to stay compliant with Canadian laws. Of course on LinkedIn we can't target thousands of people quickly but on the flipside we get much higher quality leads.

How We Integrate Small Business Dream With LinkedIn

Small Business Dream has many functions. One, is it's perfect for keeping track and reminding you of who you've contacted, how they have responded, and most importantly reminds you of when you need to follow up again, and once you have populated a follow up series, can even suggest what you may want to say to them next.

Semi-automatic vs. Automated

At Small Business Dream, we don't believe in sending spammy automated messages to your contacts or prospects. With our software, we are able to customize the messages depending on what they write back, personalizing it to fit the recipient and circumstances.

For example:

Mon

Hey Dennis. Thanks for reaching out. I was in a very recent auto accident and needed surgery so sorry for not responding earlier. I am drugged up on pain killers that zonk me out until I am able to be mobile again. I am not home with my computer but I do not use a lot of software automation tools. Have you found any info in recent academia papers or contacted business associations? Small business- employees up to 100? (You may need to define that) I would do some Google searches and find top software tool companies to contact as they may have done market research that they will share.

10:16 PM

Hi [redacted], sorry to hear about your accident and wish you a speedy recovery. Thank you for sharing your information with me. I was just reading an article which caused me to write a blog post on the value of customer data. Not sure if you are interested or not, but here is a handy link to it on Pulse http://twt.bz/smdr. I would LOVE to hear your opinion on it.

10:40 PM

Wouldn't it be terrible if the message was automated? If you were just automating your messaging campaign you would have just bypassed this contact's horrific accident and seemed like a complete idiot. Through a semi-automated process, we still had the bulk of the message ready to send but were able to sympathize with her and let her know we actually were paying attention to her and her response to our initial semi-automated message. That's how you form great customer relationships. It's not just about pushing your agenda.

If you sent a prospect a message and didn't even acknowledge the accident, all trust would be broken and you wouldn't have any chance of making the sale.

Even when we mess up the message by putting in the wrong name we were able to quickly correc

Apr 12

Hey Megan , thank you for connecting with me on LinkedIn. I am doing some market research on software tools small business owners and managers use in their business for CRM, Sales and Marketing Automation, and Email Marketing Automation. Would you be so kind as to share what tools you have found to be good?

4:35 AM

Hi Dennis, my name is [redacted] not Megan. Not sure if you meant this question for me. I usually work on enterprise scale applications. I don't use these kinds of tools other than what we use in our company Yammer, Salesforce.
Best
Camille

7:10 AM

Hi I apologize for typing in wrong name. and Thank you for sharing the information. I was just reading an article which caused me to write a blog post on the value of customer data. Not sure if you are interested or not, but here is a handy link to it on Pulse http://twt.bz/smdr. I would LOVE to hear your opinion on it.

6:38 PM

t it as you can see below:

Why is this important? Because everybody knows all about automation tools out there and they can smell them from a mile away. People will forgive you if you use the wrong name, especially if you apologize; but they won't if you keep sending them automated messages without even acknowledging them as a person.

Our Results

With our cold outreach program, we decided to play the long game by developing long-term customer relationships rather than go straight for the sale. We don't feel outright pitching our CRM was the right approach and most people don't take too kindly to it on LinkedIn (or any other platform for that matter). Instead we went for the soft sell to see what sort of CRM they used and if they didn't have one or were unhappy with their current one, we could gradually introduce them to Small Business Dream.

One of the things we wanted to gage was the response rate, which we found extremely positive. Whereas typical cold emails get a response rate of 1%-10%, depending on who you ask, we got a response rate of about 45%. Although we didn't reach thousands of people which you can do in a typical cold email blast, we found, by having a laser-focused semi-automated system, we could be more effective in reaching more key customers and influencers.

Now these are hardly scientific numbers, but we were happy with the response we got and we could learn more about our customers which in turn makes us better at selling to them.

Hi Dennis,

My pleasure. Thanks for the approach.

I have a boutique consultancy firm and currently use none of the aforementioned tools. However, if you decide to update your research later, I might be able to respond in the future as I'm planning to diversify my activity that must use some of the above tools.

If it is possible to share your report results, I'd be interested to learn more about it.

8:19 AM

Today

Sorry its been a few weeks since we connected. Thank you sharing information. I was just reading an article which caused me to write a blog post on the value of customer data. Not sure if you are interested or not, but here is a handy link to it on Pulse http://twt.bz/smdr. I would LOVE to hear your opinion on it.

And we were able to move customers down the sales pipeline by meeting them in person or talking to them over the phone.

Hey [redacted] thank you for connecting with me on LinkedIn. I am doing some market research on software tools small business owners and managers use in their business for CRM, Sales and Marketing Automation, and Email Marketing Automation. Would you be so kind as to share what tools you have found to be good?

10:48 PM

Tue

I'm a fan of simple and easy to use CRM

6:06 AM

Today

Hi [redacted] do you currently use a CRM?

6:53 AM

We all use different level of CRM but let see what you're offering and who is the ideal client. Why not coming to my business mastermind tomorrow morning at 7:30 am in downtown and we get to know more about your work

8:07 AM

Through our research, we've established using Small Business Dream with LinkedIn is a great way of garnishing new leads. With our software, it only takes a couple of minutes a day to see who you need to contact, where they are in the sequence, and adjust the message based on the response. With a 45% response rate, we were able to quickly lead the prospect through the sales pipeline.

Imagine 10 minutes per day doing linked in prospecting, should allow you to attempt connection with 10 to 20 people. Let's go low and say only 10 per day and you get 40% response, so 4 people per day connect back to you and you being to get to know each other. In a month that is 120 qualified prospects in your pipeline. What if you sold to 10% of them…? What is your average sale per client? Would that change your profitability? Do YOU have 10 minutes per day to learn the SmallBizDream LinkedIn lead generation program?

PART III: SALES

SALES EXPERTS SALES PIPELINE SECRETS

In the last twenty years, business has changed the way they deal with potential customers and are now adopting a subtler approach to convert their leads into sales. Unlike traditional methods like the ones used in outbound marketing, it involved several stages, carefully structured and monitored to maximize the potential of converting every lead – also known as a soft sales approach.

This process of getting your leads to become customers is best represented by your sales pipeline and sales funnel. Sales pipeline can be viewed in different ways but the basic idea is the same: "How do I get my leads from point A to point B, and where does the money go in all of those stages?" How much of it can I automate or semi-automate?

What Are the Stages in a Sales Pipeline?

By the time your customers reached the point of buying your products and services, they would have gone through different stages in your sales pipeline. We can see this even in day to day transactions.

For instance, you are watching a football game and this guy selling hotdogs passed by the aisle. When you start getting interested with one of those (because they look appetizing) and the guy offers you two for the price of one, you are now in their sales pipeline and by the time you reach the end you will be one of his happy customers.

Companies differ as to the exact number of stages to keep a sales pipeline running smoothly. However, most companies would agree that six to seven stages hit the sweet spot. We will briefly go through each stage and see how the experts deal with it.

Stage 1: Generating Leads. One of the most successful ways to generate more leads is through social media, website content, freebies, giveaways, and social events. You are not concerned about making the sales just yet. You just want people to get interested in what you have. SEO and SEM strategies is one of the best ways to generate more leads by improving traffic to your website and get better search rankings. A good sales funnel set up in Small Business Dream can really help you shortcut and automate this process.

Stage 2: Maintaining Interest through Follow Ups. After giving away some of your goodies through your website or social media account, give them value without any strings attached. They will then trust you with their email address. In fact, they will be more than happy to subscribe to your newsletter and answer your survey. Offer more content, something they would enjoy watching or reading, anything they can use right away. Setting up an email automation software and auto-responder like those in Small Business Dream is extremely useful at this stage. Pretty soon, they will get hooked, and by then they would be ready for the next step.

Stage 3: Getting the Right Information. Now you've locked on to your target, it's time to take a step further and get you closer to your goal which is to turn them into your loyal customers. We don't do the selling part just yet. Some email marketers make the mistake of pushing their products too early. We don't want to make an impression that we are too desperate to win the sale (needy is creepy). Just ask some basic information about your subscriber to help you with the next stage which will qualify them for potential sales. Survey forms can do the job quite well.

Stage 4: Qualifying Prospects. At this point we are now trying to assess the possibility of your leads becoming an opportunity for creating sales. Based on the information gathered though surveys, which includes his or her specific interests, sex, occupation, income etc., we can start the process of qualifying that prospect, the result of which will determine if we can move that prospect closer to the end of the sales pipeline.

Stage 5: Assigning Lead Scores. By this time, you'll have a clearer picture of who your prospects are. You can give each prospect a lead score or priority which will determine how much time you want to spend on each lead. Consequently, those with higher scores are given more priority while those at the lower end can be recycled at any stage in the sales pipeline or funnel.

Stage 6: Closing the Deal. The customer finally agrees and the sale is made. Try to gain more from it by up-selling or cross-selling to your customers. Some sales pipelines include post-sale stage where customers are encouraged to patronize their product through constant follow-ups and having them sign up for loyalty or point cards.

Maintaining a Healthy Sales Pipeline

Maintaining a steady flow of leads, opportunities, and sales is critical in any business. If at any stage the sales pipeline gets bogged down and fail to meet their goals, the company could take a hit and it will seriously affect their bottom line. Some ways to keep the sales pipeline in good shape includes:

1. Checking your conversion rates
2. Making constant improvements
3. Keeping an eye on your sales cycle.
4. Holding regular sales pipeline meetings.

HOW TO BE A SALES PROFESSIONAL

The sales profession is not for the faint at heart. If anything, it's one of the toughest jobs a person can do, albeit the most rewarding one in terms of incentives and overall income as well. Surviving in this kind of job demands persistent effort and a high degree of salesmanship, something that only comes through years of experience and proper training.

Sales reps are constantly under pressure to perform within the company's standard. Attrition rate in the sales department is fairly high, as much as 50% a year in some companies. Most of the time, salespeople may resort to desperate measures like discounts or other margin lowering concepts in a last-ditch effort to reach the monthly or weekly quota. As we know these futile attempts often make no difference whatsoever other than making them look desperate and reducing overall corporate margins.

Beyond the BIGGEST problem sales people suffer from which is the lack of proper and timely follow up, one of the roadblocks to becoming a successful salesperson is the lack of proper understanding of the sales process and dealing with customers. In order to succeed in a highly competitive market, a salesperson should know the difference between persistence and pushing too far.

There are some telltale signs a salesperson has already crossed the line:

The salesperson does all the talking. You might have

experienced this yourself as a customer when you walked inside the mall. The sales rep would come to you with a lot of enthusiasm, eager to show you what they have and assume you want it after they do all the talking.

The second mistake a salesperson often makes is offering solutions prematurely. We know businesses exist to answer customer's specific needs or provide solution to their 'pain points'. If they offer something that has real value to the customer, it wouldn't be too hard to make the sale. Unfortunately, what usually happens is salesperson will jump right in and offer a solution (their products and services) to the customer without even knowing the circumstances behind the customer's need or problem. Wouldn't it be better if they got to know the customer first and perhaps know a thing or two about them and their needs before suggesting a solution? That way they will sound genuinely interested in solving the customers problem and not just looking for his hard-earned cash.

Salespeople get too 'salesy'. Nobody likes a pushy salesperson and people's natural reaction is to back away if a sales person tries to tell the prospect what is good for them, even if the prospect wants what the salesperson is selling. Be honest about your product or service and never over promise and definitely never lie. A salesperson needs to lead the prospect to water, not try to drown them.

Another common problem is a salesperson offers a discount too soon. When a sales rep offers discounts right off the bat or tell the customers they offer the 'cheapest' or 'low-priced' items, it could be they're not selling enough and they need to have them sold as quickly as possible. Although it might sound good on the surface, it could actually send a different message to the customers. When the price is instantly discounted at the first sign of buyer objection, it could mean three things: it's bad quality', had lost its quality, or it's overpriced. Either way, customers will have a negative impression about the offer, especially those who prefer quality and value over price savings.

Sometimes a salesperson will punch below the belt' by badmouthing the competition. This perhaps is one of the worst things a salesperson can do just to get the sale or discourage the customer to go elsewhere. Talking badly about other brands shows a lack of confidence in one's own products and services and shows an unsportsmanlike attitude that could undermine a company's reputation. If what the company offers is really good, what's the need to criticize or insult others in front of customers?

The notion of a smooth-talking salesman being able to sell shoddy goods is long gone. It's no longer just about the personality or creating a good first impression though it is still very important. We live in a new era where customers make buying decisions based on facts and not just on some 30-second TV, or YouTube commercial. We don't expect customers to just pour in from a simple well-done ad or video. We need to cultivate their minds and educate them about the benefits of using our products or services instead of pushing them down their throats with great "closing" techiniques. Identify a problem to solve or a need to fill, and sell to those who have the problem or need.

There are 3 things you can do to help accomplish this:

Know your customers better. It's okay to set a goal as to the number of closed deals or sales per month. In fact, most companies encourage (or require) their sales rep to do this to be qualified for promotion and not be labeled as underperforming. But moving randomly from one potential unqualified prospect to another will only lead to frustration. You need a tool that allows you to keep in touch with multiple leads at a time and be able to continue to qualify them based on their merits or lead scores. This ensures every effort is well worth it – no wasted time or effort. CRM tools like smallbizdream.com can make all this possible with very little effort and at a very minimal cost after initial signup.

Your initial contact with your customers can get you clues about their interest and preferences. If you are so fortunate, don't hesitate to offer a targeted follow up where warranted, or a free subscription to your newsletter to keep them updated in general with your company, product and/or services. Have them fill a quick survey and ask for the most basic contact information like their name, mobile number and/or email address.

An automated or semi-automated system to respond to their survey responses is extremely valuable at this point. Responses will vary with every prospect but the important thing is to prioritize high quality leads first.

Except for the odd time you get lucky, you won't get the sale on the first engagement. On average, it takes around 7 engagements before a deal is made. Some go so far in this social media age to say it takes as many as 14. Be patient and wait for the right opportunity. You don't want to annoy your prospect with your incessant calls or reminders about the offer. But if your leads are already ripe for the picking, by all means get to them and seal the deal as soon as possible. It is all about balance, but constant reaching out an touching in multiple ways is the key to that balance.

It's good to know sales people don't have to look desperate to achieve their goals with a good CRM and Sales and Marketing Automation in place. Small Business Dream offers sales, marketing, and email automation software for sales reps and small business owners at a very minimal cost. It even starts for FREE up to 2000 communications per month.

THE DEADLIEST ERROR IN ANY TYPE OF SALES

I have been selling professionally since I was 10 years old. Yes, that's right 10! It all started with pet rocks. I got a rock polishing machine for Christmas one year, found a bunch of unused bottlecaps, and bought some googly eyes. Those components and a bit of silicone glue and adorable pet rocks were born!

I didn't even consider prejudging at that age. When you're young, you aren't jaded. I just went door to door to door, and made a small fortune— at least in a 10-year old's' eyes —selling Pet Rocks for $1 each.

Later, I moved onto delivering newspapers, selling annual newspaper subscriptions, and new subscriptions. Yep, I got the free trip to Disneyland selling the Edmonton Journal newspaper when I was 12 years old! Keep in mind 6 others who matched me hour for hour out canvassing did not. What was the difference? Luck?

I did this by using the puppy dog close. Of course, I had no idea it was called the puppy dog close when I was doing it back then, but it proved very effective. This was the line I used as I neared my goal and time was running short back then: "I just need 5 more subscribers and I get a free trip to Disneyland. If you would just help me out, I would be happy to send you a Postcard from Disneyland."

I sent 5 postcards! I still hadn't learned to prejudge. I had upped my game, I think the subscriptions were about $30 whole dollars a year!

I then ran my own Neon Sign company. It is here where I

learned to prejudge. I was old enough to have heard enough 'no's' and 'not interested'. It was here where I learned to FIGHT THE URGE to pre-judge. It was here the idea was born, long before the technology and internet existed to build a piece of software like Small Business Dream. We used a product called PackRat, which was good at the time but not exactly what I wanted.

Slowly, I started to pre-judge by the tone of the potential customer's voice on the phone. Or the fact they didn't call me back.

I even played the old, "it is Monday" game, nobody wants to be followed up on Monday. They are all too busy. I was deep in my pre-judging mode.

At this time, I was selling Neon Signs anywhere from $299 to $10,000. It seems the prejudging happens more and more often the higher ticket item you sell.

The battle NEVER ends for a salesperson.

Now I sell $10,000 to $180,000 Software systems as well as FREE and paid licenses of Small Business Dream. I would love to say I have learned to NOT pre-judge. I can tell you I have found a way to limit how much I do it.

It is called Small Business Dream. It simply works by giving me a list of people to call based upon MY decided order by the last contact I had with them.

Open Small Business Dream, call, email, send a text, send a Facebook message, or whatever else it tells me to do, and don't stop until the list is empty. Systemize. Not 100% magic but keeps me on track a lot more than just hoping I will remember who to call and what was said and NOT make excuses they maybe aren't interested so don't call.

Check out the video at twt.bz/prejudge

Just CALL or DO the action Small Business Dream gives me.

At least I have a weapon against my brain!

Is the battle over?

About two weeks ago, I got a phone call on a Sunday morning from somebody interested in our software, and they only were going to have a very small number of people in their company, and I totally PREJUDGED thinking they weren't a prospect. It was Sunday morning, so I think I was a little miffed at myself that I answered the phone on a Sunday morning to begin with.

I did all the wrong things in sales; I answered the phone in a slightly less than perfect mindset. I PREJUDGED this wasn't a prospect and I had wasted my time. Fortunately, I use SMALL BUSINESS DREAM, so he was already in the system and he came up for a call-back on Monday.

With the help of Small Business Dream, I could battle against my own BRAIN'S poor judgement. I ended up calling him back and following up as I was supposed to ON MONDAY, even though I had completely prejudged him on Sunday.

Well, guess what? It turned out we were to have another call the next day and I felt he was very likely going to purchase our $30,000 software platform from me. The key in sales is DON'T PREJUDGE. Even the best salespersons aren't perfect. I got the sale the very next day.

I prejudged and could have lost the sale but thankfully I got lucky and saved it, because I had proper sales automation in place to make sure I stayed in communication, even though I didn't feel like it, and it was hard to pick up the phone to call.

Small Business Dream said I need to call him, and my stats for the day said I had only made 61 contacts so far that day. My goal was 100. I couldn't handle the pressure of resisting the call, and everything just forced me to pick up the phone to make that last phone call and sent that last text message.

And I got the SALE, if I was my own company's commissioned salesperson, I would have earned $1000 for that call!

DON'T PREJUDGE, just let your sales process take hold and do the right things according to the setttings you made in your sales automation follow-up software, when you were thinking clearly, vs. how heavy the phone looked at the time of needing to take action. By not prejudging, you are going to sell more and make a ton more money.

4 WAYS TO BECOME AN EMAIL MARKETING NINJA!

Despite the many methods of marketing and selling through social media, ultimately generating an email marketing list as you go is still king of the road.

It's what drives a lot of businesses, both online and offline. It's the best direct selling tool businesses have today. If you're not using email to communicate and sell to your customers then why the heck not?

It's probably because you've never really considered the power of a consistent, follow up automated, or semi-automated email sequences. Or maybe you don't know how. It's actually far easier than you might think.

But first let's take you back a bit. . .

I'm going to take you back to the time you were overjoyed when you got email. There was that ping of anticipation, the little swirly icon, and then you'd click on it, and wait for it to open.

Unfortunately, that's no longer the case. Fast forward to now. Answering emails is probably the last thing you want to do.

The average person gets eight-four emails a day. That's not including social media interactions like Facebook Messages, LinkedIn Messages, Tweets, Snap- chats, and whatever else there is at the time you read this book. There are probably a million things you prefer to do then wade through email wasteland!

It's almost impossible to respond to eight-four messages a day, let alone read them, so you must be a marketing ninja to stand out. You just need to train to do those backflips and karate chops!

How do you do that? I'm glad you asked. Luckily, I've come up with several things you can do to become a master.

Strategy

Before you send a single email, you need an overall strategy. Like anything else, if you fly by the seat of your pants then you're not going to be effective. You have to always ask how it benefits your audience. What message are you trying to send? How many audiences do you need to address? What are the forks in your sales process? Take your time to stop and think about your approach and execution.

Start by listing all the Types of follow up you want to do:

1. Product/Service interest
2. After purchase
3. General Newsletter
4. Specific Newsletters

Next identify the forks

For example, let's say the third email or communication through social media gave your General Newsletter subscriber the opportunity to take a short survey. In that survey they went from general interest to interest specifically in one of your products or services. This would cause you to want to take them OUT of your general newsletter and add them to a more SPECIFIC newsletter/follow-up, OR possibly leave them in the General newsletter AND supplement them with more information by either email, SMS, Social media etc.

These forks are critical to making your email list earn you the biggest return. The old days of everyone in the same boring automated and automated sounding generic email follow up are dead.

Once you have identified your Forks, write down the action you want them to take. You should strategize at least three months in advance and know exactly what you want to say in each case. The more effort you put into setting up your Automation properly, the bigger the returns you will generate on it. As your business changes, it's possible to change your strategy but as they say 'fail to plan then plan to fail.'

Content

Obviously, the content of your email series' and or social media communications is the most important part of your follow up. Starting with your subject line. If your emails are boring or too salesy nobody is going to read them.

I know, the truth hurts sometimes, but if you slowly educate your customers to your awesomeness and your writing is entertaining then you'll have prospects salivating over your email content.

Personalization

The more you know about your email list the better and more 'valuable' it is. The more you can customize it to a specific prospect or group of prospects the better. If you know a particular prospect likes a certain beer, you can craft a message around it. The same for coffee, restaurants or sports. Segmented lists and dynamic content shows your audience you've thought about their needs and care about building a personal relationship with them, even if it's automated or semi-automated which we will get into next.

There are a couple ways of segmenting your email list. You can send your existing list a survey and then record those responses. You can create different landing pages, each with a different message. Or you can run different contests to see which people respond to. Get creative!

Automation

This is by far my favorite tip. I love automation but maybe love semi-automation even more! Why? It makes life so much easier. Why do all the work over and over again when you only have to do it once? How often do you copy and paste emails feeling excited how much time you are saving. Proper automation allows you to not even need to do that cut and past.

How often do you cut and paste, but just add a line or two to make it specific to your target? Hmm… not automation, but you just nailed semi-automation. What if you had a system that enabled you to do that more efficiently?

Your customers won't know the difference unless you do it poorly. Remember to personalize it! (Hint we just talked about it!) If you personalize and segment your list correctly, then your customer will feel special and privileged.

Remember the key to good sales automation is it NOT BEING DETECTED by your target! This means your content has to be written in a personal manner, NOT stuffy over professional.

There are many ways to do this. Most email marketing companies have a way you can create auto responders that will automatically trigger when you add somebody to a list. This means a series of emails going out on a timed basis. The content and timing is set by you in advance, then once a person is added they get email 1, then in xx days they get email 2 etc. All content and timing is set up by you initially.

Small Business Dream (smallbizdream.com) goes just a step further with autoresponders. It allows you to set up a Semi-Automated email series. This means as you login each day, it give you a list of ALL you need to send a particular semi-automated email you set up. You get the ability to add a custom sentence or two to the general content one email at a time before you send them. This creates enormous response rates when compared with simple fully automated series. Well worth the extra 15 to 20 seconds per email on a super targeted list.

Make sure you track your results. See your open rates, click through rates, survey response rates. See what people respond to the best. Remember the more you can learn about your customers through automation and categorize as you go, the easier it is to sell to them after.

With only 39% of retailers sending personalized product information to their customers there is obviously great room for improvement! Just by adding good email strategy and follow up, you can double or triple your sales! More about this in the following chapter.

Get More Responses to Your Email by Following This Simple Rule

Getting people to talk with you is especially hard in a fast-paced environment. Getting them to talk with you through email is even harder. However, just by knowing what makes your clients tick and providing tangible value in EVERY communication increases the chances of people reading and responding to your emails.

Notice the word 'with'. We're not sending out emails en masse just to get our voices heard but we're trying to start and engage in a meaningful conversation with our potential customers. Hint: there's actually a way to automate these tasks without your clients knowing it – and it's definitely not spamming.

Email DOs and DON'Ts

First things first, here are a few Dos and Don'ts to keep in mind to avoid the dreaded spam filter:

DON'Ts:

Don't send unsolicited emails. Some email services have an auto feature which sends unsolicited emails directly to the spam folder (this feature can be tweaked by the user). Your spam folder could already have dozens of emails from people you don't know or companies you didn't sign-up for.

Don't use deceptive subject lines. It's not just wrong, it's also illegal in some countries. You or your company could be fined for misleading your recipients just with the subject line alone (CAN-SPAM Act of 2003 specifically relating to Canadian customers) which is much worse than having your mails dumped to the spam folder.

Don't use spam or phishing words or phrases. There are certain words and phrases that trigger spam filter in some email services. These are not 100% fool-proof systems and sometimes even innocuous subject titles with the words 'congratulations' or 'free' can be labeled as spam.

DOs:

Use a double opt-in strategy. Your safest bet to is to set up a system that encourages your visitors to sign up to your newsletter, then confirming by email they wanted to signup.

Having landing pages with meaningful surveys for your company and products.

Time your emails wisely. Frequency can vary depending on the type of email your sending and how responsive your recipients are, and the quality of the list. The rule of the thumb when it comes to email intervals is the more your email gets read or replied to by the receiver, the more frequent your emails should be. Be careful not to 'over-mail'. Research have shown 73% of 'unsubscribes' as a result of 'over-mailing'.

Use semi-automation for emails vs full email automation as soon as you have qualified a prospect into a lead with your general email newsletter or website.

Offer an opt-out option. Having an opt-out link in your email conveys your truthfulness and carries a sense of no obligation to your recipients. Just in case they chose not to hear from you anymore, this is actually a better option than having your emails ending up in spam.

What makes people WANT to read your emails?

Making people read or even respond to your emails is both a sciencc and an art. We have to understand how people react to a given stimulus, what drives them, what makes them tick, and a host of other things related to human psychology. On the other hand, it's also an art which gets better with time as one applies his own creative genius and aesthetics in the art of communication. For those that are not that creative, you can just test test test and watch your results to see which of your communications are doing better than others.

We'll go through a typical marketing email format and dissect its parts one by one.

Subject Title

The title accounts for 33% of mails actually read by their recipients. In other words just by improving the subject title can make big difference whether or not your prospect will read on or hit the delete button. Experience tells us the optimum length for a subject title is around 7-10 words or around 30-40 characters. Make it count by using call-to-action (CTA) words and arousing their curiosity (if they just came to your landing page or met with you in person, that should give you enough clues).

Example: "Hey, Tim, here's an awesome tip for your small business."

Opening Line

Once you've found an audience, go straight to the point without sounding like an old-fashioned salesman. Nobody likes a stuffed shirt. Forget your accomplishments, your amazing company, technology, widget, president, degree, award etc. for a moment and concentrate on establishing rapport and providing VALUE.

Remember, "People don't care how much you know until they know how much your care." The reader should feel relaxed – as if talking to a friend.

Example: "I'm excited to know we both have something in common. I'd like to share with you some tips that might help you:

Body

Based on experience, people won't spend too much time reading their emails. They just want to know what you have to say, and particularly, **what's in it for them**. Three to four paragraphs should be the maximum.

Others find the inverted pyramid useful (the same technique used in news writing) because it encourages readers to keep going right to the end of your letter. Whenever appropriate use bullet points and italics to emphasize your points. Be concise and to the point and don't forget the main point is giving VALUE not selling.

If your readers have come this far and are reading your emails and responding to them, congratulations. All you need now is to wrap things up with a powerful and compelling call-to-action statement.

Aim for a definitive response like asking them for a follow-up, scheduling an appointment call or meeting up in person. If they do agree for a follow-up offer something as an incentive for coming back like insider information about the company, exclusive access to research, reports, white paper, and other relevant information about your product or service.

CRM apps are pretty good at doing follow-ups which is why most companies invest in a good CRM service including a sales funnel, and sales and marketing automation. Usually, it takes 4 to 7 engagements before you can finally talk about business which is perfectly okay and NORMAL in today's social media world.

Any kind of marketing strategy involving email and regular follow-ups with contacts won't be complete without the right sales and marketing tools to get the job done. (shameless plug, smallbizdream.com free for up to 2000 communications per month is a great one)

The good thing about having the right CRM for your business is you'll never miss communicating with any of your contacts whether by email, social media, or telephone (gasp!) as your CRM tells you when the next communication is due and when the time is right to follow up and close the deal.

SIMPLE WAYS TO INCREASE YOUR WEBSITE SALES

Everybody knows your website is your storefront so it's astounding how many people don't give it regular upkeep – a fresh coat of paint, new signage, and a good cleaning now and then.

As technology such as screen sizes, faster internet and mobile phones change, there comes implied expectations from your customers your website keeps up with all the latest trends.

Your website represents your brand even when you're not around. It markets you 24/7, even when you're asleep. If you have a good website that is visually appealing, well-written copy, and a good call to action you can significantly increase your sales and your bottom line.

You might think you know what your customer wants, but do you really? Instead of assuming you know, why not listen to the customer and ask questions to find out what it is he/she REALLY wants.

1. **Tell your customers about benefits, not features.**

Let's take a car as an example. Perhaps it has a 300-horse power engine, leather seats, and four-wheel drive. Those would all be features.

Those things are all great but they are not the reason people buy cars. Benefits are being are being about to accelerate quickly, being comfortable while driving and being able to maneuver in the snow.

Your customers don't want to know the ins and outs of your features, they want to know it can benefit them! Save the details of the product for a secondary page on your website, or perhaps a product page. You can give some main selling points, but keep the minor details off the home page. This spot should be for benefits of your products and or services – what is in it for your customer.

For example, let's say you've got a strategy to get your clients out of debt. Don't give them the nuts and bolts of how it works on the front page, give them the abbreviated version, and save the small print for another page. Tell them instead how they can imagine some of the specific benefits of a life with ample funds and freedom from debt. Would that get YOUR attention if the shoe was on the other foot?

1. Keep communication consistent with potential buyers.

Most marketing experts say it takes between five and seven views of your products or services to turn your leads into a customer. They're obviously interested if they've managed to get to your site and request information, especially if they're checking you out 7+ times! So why not keep them informed about your news and updates to the site? You just may have a future customer.

It's also a good practice to use a "bookmark this page" and "tell a friend about this page" tool, making it easier to get potential buyers for the future. Even if they're not immediately buying, it doesn't mean they won't be back!

2. Encourage your site visitors to ask questions.

Some people may think they're bothering you or wasting your time to ask you a question. Extend your virtual arms to each and every visitor that comes into your site, and encourage them to ask questions!

If you see the same question coming from those visitors over and over again, you might want to consider a "FAQ" page, which keeps your visitors from having to ask the same questions over and over again. It not only makes your customer happy to be able to find their own answers it will save your company money in answering phone calls or emails for the same question over and over.

3. **Make the buying experience easier. Don't ask for information that you don't need.**

Ask for the bare minimum information from the customer so they can "get in, and get out". Then later on, you can send them a quick thank you note and a follow up to see how they liked your website. If you do need a LOT of information to properly qualify them, use a Step or Squeeze survey format. Ask a few simple questions, then based upon some key answers, direct them to give you MORE information as you acknowledge their previous answer and WHY you need more information to help them.

No Hoops.

Don't make your customer jump through hoops to buy your products. It will only frustrate them, and make them put off buying for later - and later may never come!

Have multiple calls to action.

Figure out what you want your customer to do and then have multiple ways of telling them to do exactly that! It may seem like a no-brainer but I'm constantly surprised at how must websites fail to persuade their prospect to fill in a form or call, or request a callback—whatever action it is you want your customer to do. Your call to action should also be on each page of your website so at any point your prospect can take the action you want.

7. **Use a good CRM tool to help keep customers in the loop with your business.**

Utilizing a good Customer Relationship Tool goes a long way to keeping you organized when it comes to communicating with your customers. If you've got a sale or special on your products or services that you want them to know about (and they should), your CRM is an invaluable way to bring customers BACK to your business with the click of a button.

Going one step further, utilizing a powerful mobile customer relationship tool will allow you to keep in touch with those valuable customers on the fly!

By keeping these lines of communication open with your site visitors and potential customers, you'll find it easy to gain more trust and credibility with them and, in turn, more sales!

WHY NOT TO FORGET YOUR PREVIOUS CUSTOMERS

One of the best ways to get new customers, is to stay connected with those you've already done business with. I know that sounds crazy, but it's the truth. You may wonder why do you want to spend time or energy on people you've already sold to? Why waste your time?

Simple! Your current – and even your previous customers – are the lifeblood of your business.

As you get each new customer, you want to communicate with that customer again in the future to keep your business in their mind, and to keep them on as a walking and talking billboard for your business.

The most powerful type of marketing is referral marketing.

The future of your business needs to evolve to include repeat customers and referred customers, both of whom are vital to the ongoing relationship of your business, the consumer, and the local surroundings of your business.

So now you ask; "How can I communicate with previous customers without it sounding forced?" It's easier than you might think!

Even if your customers are online, you can still communicate with them. Social media and the internet make it easier than ever before to reach out to your customers. A simple Facebook message or email may be enough to re-establish the relationship. Add previous customers to your favorites list on social media.

Refer to them by name, and offer helpful, metered MEANINGFUL and HELPFUL advice not just SALESY STUFF.

Chat with your customers about the care and maintenance of what they have purchased from you, or the work you have done for them. Ask if there is anything that can be done to improve the process they went through while dealing with your business.

You can network with your clients by taking them to lunch, or doing something out of the 'ordinary' to express your appreciation for their business. As you continue to acknowledge those clients, they'll keep you fresh in their minds. They'll tell others about how you thanked them, and how they feel about your business.

The internet business is, of course, going to use newsletters, emails and special offers sent to previous customers as ways of communicating and keeping in touch with those customers. It's always a good idea to wave your hands in the air and say: "I'm here, don't forget about me" Keeping the lines of communication open with a customer or previous customer is going to increase awareness of your products and services. This in turn is going to increase sales, one repeat customer at a time.

In business, you can communicate with previous customers by creating mailing lists and using these mailing lists coupled with a great CRM to stay in touch. Offering helpful tips about the care and maintenance of a product they purchased with you, or making helpful recommendations for its use are great ways to stay in touch, and your customer will greatly appreciate the effort.

Make sure these types of communications are very micro focused and 80% value to the customer, less than 20% corporate mumbo jumbo salesly stuff.

Be sure to communicate with your previous customers in the

way they have suggested they prefer, whether that be SMS or txt message, FB Messenger, WhatsApp, WeChat, LinkedIn, phone call, and even just email. (always try to get email address to build a list even when they are ALSO getting communications by other methods)

Small Business Dream (smallbizdream.com) can help you keep all these types of follow up straight, organized and efficient.

HOW TO NETWORK LIKE A BOSS

Do you go to networking events? If you're a business owner, you definitely should be.

It seems the higher up somebody is in an organization, the more likely they feel going to a networking event is kind of a "dirty" thing or a waste of time just because they don't see immediate results. Sometimes it can take years for a particular networking event to pay off.

Some people just aren't comfortable with networking events. It makes them feel a little too salesy and they're doing something wrong because most people are doing them wrong. The idea of a networking event is to make friends first. You think to yourself "Oh my god! Build relationships. Sounds hard." You don't just go and vomit your corporate information all over people. You go to form relationships.

You are obviously looking to steer the conversation in a way to see if they might be a potential client, but you need people to know, like, and trust you before they will become a client.

When I go to a networking event, I break down people into a couple of categories, depending on who the person is. The categories are usually potential friend, potential client, potential employee, and potential partner. Just because someone starts out as a friend doesn't mean they can't become a client or a partner later on. Your relationship may change. Or maybe you'll just remain really good golf buddies.

Whoever they are, you should put them into an automated follow up series for personal contact, so you're still interacting with them, even if you haven't actually gone to the point of figuring out where they might fit into your business or where you might fit into theirs.

Then you segment into business categories. For example, I put those interested in a free trial of SmallBizDream in one category, those interested in becoming a reseller in another, or those interested in becoming a consultant in yet another. All of this is learned in a carefully crafted conversation.

You go into a networking function armed with your conversation you practiced and rehearsed. You've seen how people react to things in their face and body language when you talk to them.

You get to the point where you're a broken record which is GREAT because broken records work! Then you can get even better.

This is practicing the kick 10,000 times instead of a new kick every time. The more you do it, the easier it gets.

I've worked through a million iterations. If you want to network like a boss you do it by going to four or five events a week. Not four or five a month. Not four or five a year. Go to four or five a week, and within three weeks you will have honed your skills. You will have totally sucked in front of a whole bunch of people, but with all the practice you will have improved.

The great part is everyone gets nervous, especially the first few times. "Oh yeah, but what if I see the guy again and he knows I sucked?" Guess what I found happened? They overhear you at another event and they'll come up to you and say, "Damn you've gotten so much better than the first day I met you!" Everyone's there playing the same game. We're all trying to improve our skills. We're all trying to squeak out a living while helping others solve problems. We're all trying to enjoy the surf, the sun, and whatever.

Somehow, we just have to get people to stop sweating the details. If you're out there generating prospects and leads stop sweating the details! Go with the idea you've helped some people. Go with the idea maybe at the networking event you can point some people to some helpful resources. Or you can introduce them to someone else you know that might make a good relationship or maybe you can introduce them to a free trial of a couple of tools you found.

Go there with the idea you're going to go to this networking event, and you're going to help a few people with problems in their business. If that turns into a sale than great. Don't be selfish and only try to help people with problems your product sells. Just help people. For example, someone's struggling with taking a picture with their cell phone." "Hey, something I can help you with?"

I love networking events for that reason. It's incredibly fast to rapidly iterate. The business prospects are all there. You're not going to close a business prospect the first time you meet them at a networking event, so stop trying and you'll have way more fun.

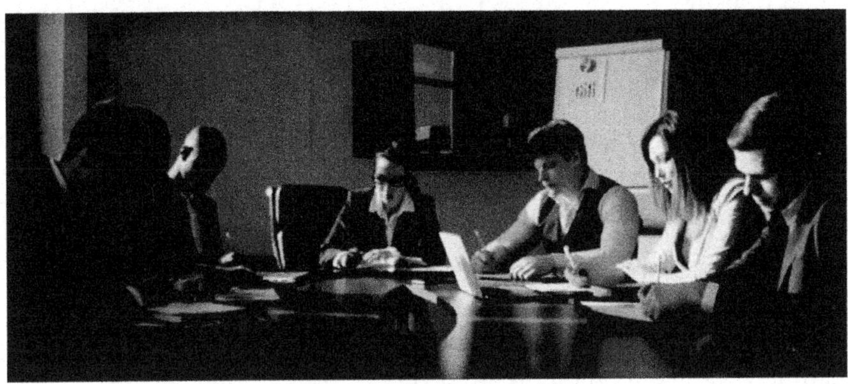

Check out the video at twt.bz/networking

You need to build a relationship and have that conversation. They need to see you a couple of times to build trust. You show up to a networking event once and you go, "Well that didn't work." That's not how networking works. You need to practice.

There's always going to be ways you can improve. If you do fail, then of course you know there's lots of ways you can reframe that. You should practice thinking your identity and your role as separate. You can think: "They're not rejecting me. They're rejecting my role."

You know so many times people attach their role and identity together, and they find themselves feeling hurt, rejected and devalued.

I knew a man who worked his entire life and he eventually retired. He was a fit healthy guy when he retired but he died five years later because he actually attached his role as business owner and mayor of a town to his identity. It happens a lot. You know people lose their job and throw themselves out of a window.

Often when you go into these networking events you ask yourself, "Who am I today? How do I represent myself and be okay?" If you just take an attitude of service, then you'll be successful. I've had some clients with earth-shaking reputations and huge client lists, and I've worked myself up a little bit. "Well, how am I going to sell this person?"

Take a moment to go, and tell yourself: "Hang on. If I go in with an attitude of service I can ask better questions." I can understand their business, pain, and issues better than if I gone in to try to sell something. Then you ask them: "What result would you like out of this event?"

They tell me. Guess what? I deliver what they told me they want delivered. Amazingly enough, I got the business.

I went to a networking event the other night and it's put on by one of the larger cell phone providers. It was a free event and it was fantastic. It blew my mind. It was a catered, wonderful event, and so I naturally wanted to get more involved.

I saw another one of their events come up so I'm like: "Well, I'll go. I could eat. Right?" I went there with my bucket full of bunker rings, which are my phone rings as my little Small Business Dream giveaway.

I actually went there because Rogers Mobility has just started this whole campaign to try to help small businesses and, of course, that's what we do. I went there because there was a speaker being flown in from Toronto to Vancouver.

This guy was flown in from Toronto to talk about what I talk about, so I'm like, "Hang on. I got to go meet some of these people and maybe if I get lucky I'll be able to steer the conversation to where

I can be a bit of a public speaker and get flown around Canada; helping them out and getting my message out."

It was a really hot day and I normally go to these things in a suit because I believe to always be dressed at the same or one higher than anyone you're meeting with. But I dialed it back to a polo shirt and dress slacks. When I got there everyone was at my level or a step below, so I was like, "Well, thank god I didn't show up in a suit." I would have looked better than the speaker. That's not cool.

I pulled out my bunker rings and I start talking to this nice Russian lady who was also looking at helping businesses, and she worked for a business consultant. I gave her a bunker ring. And then I'm giving out bunker rings and people are getting them and they're actually sticking them on their phones, and then this other lady comes over and she says, "You're going to be embarrassed for me when I show you what I have." She holds up her phone in her hand through this strap thing that's attached to her case. She says, "I have wanted one of those bunker rings forever."

I said, "I'll tell you what: You let me take a picture of you with that one, and then we're going to put mine on yours and we're going to take another picture. As long as you'll let me put that on Twitter and use it in my social media stuff, I'll give you one. Heck, I'll give you two."

But it turns out she was flown in from Toronto. Her sole purpose was to find energetic people who know what they're talking about to join them in speaking across Canada.

I went there to give out some bunker rings, make some friends, and eat some food and I helped this Russian lady with some of her problems in front of this other lady who's overhearing it, and suddenly she got my bunker ring. I give them to all the other executives that were in from Toronto. One guy walked away with three; apparently, he had a wife and a girlfriend.

I didn't go there and ask who's in charge and source them out. I would've sourced them out if it had developed naturally. Make no mistake about it, I would have worked the room until I found who I needed to talk to. Instead, by just being me, going there, helping people, giving away my little gizmos in a polite and respectful way that didn't interrupt their event, I was able to make the contacts I needed to.

I not only made some great contacts but I managed to get some speaking gigs out of it too. I've got the local guy wanting me to do a bunch of events that weren't as formal as that one. Then the Russian took my contact information and was very excited about collaborating with me. I've started that process and I have no doubt that once I set my mind to it it'll happen.

You do that over and over again and you'll get all the customers you could possible hope for. That's how you network like a boss. Go there to help. Go there to serve.

DIGITAL AND PHYSICAL CUSTOMER ENGAGEMENT

When the Internet was on the rise in the late 90s, it introduced a new way to engage customers which affected many large-scale industries in an unprecedented way.

Information is now getting passed from one part of the world to another at blinding speeds. More and more people are getting access to places, goods, and services once limited to a particular place or group of people. The term 'world wide web' came into existence and ushered the age of information overload.

Online stores and e-commerce started to dominate the landscape and introduced an entirely different ballgame to the marketplace. It has left a huge dent in the brick-and-mortar stores that have been around for decades.

Websites that mirror their physical stores and business establishments were set up in haste to take back what they have lost. The question is, will this digital revolution be able to replace the human aspect of customer engagement? Will there come a time when every business transaction is done entirely on automated systems and electronics without human intervention?

Two Sides of the Same Coin

The reality is digital and physical interaction with customers or are in fact two sides of the same coin. You cannot have one without the other because of their inherent strengths and weaknesses apart from each other. In the past, too much emphasis on one side has had disastrous effects and companies have to be careful enough not to fall into the same mistake. Consider the following scenario using exclusively one method of customer engagement:

Physical Customer Engagement PROS:

• Companies can communicate with customers on a much deeper level. This can be done in person, over the phone, or even through personalized emails (not to be confused with generic, marketing e-mails or automation).

• Sales people actively engage their clients in meaningful discussion by providing specific answers to customer requests, queries, and concern in a more dynamic way. Special requests and other matters relevant to the conversation are noted down for future reference and future engagements.

• It conveys the emotion and other non-verbal cues of sales and business representatives, showing their willingness and sincerity to address their client's needs (Note: it is also possible to convey one's emotion through digital customer engagements to some extent).

CONS:

• The number of man-hours necessary to carry out the job increases with the growing number of customers. It could also mean hiring additional personnel. This translates to higher running costs (hiring, training, employee benefits, etc.).

• In-person customer requests, queries and the like are slower compared to digital customer engagement. Everything is basically a one-on-one engagement. Depending on your employees' individual skill level, your customers will experience varying degrees of responsiveness. If a sales rep, for instance, is not up to speed, the customer could lose interest and the company will miss the opportunity.

Digital Customer Engagement PROS:

• Repetitive and time-consuming tasks are accomplished using CRM applications and IT services with a high level of sophistication like SmallBizDream.com.

• Significantly reduce the amount of time and resources necessary to interact and maintain customer interest through automation and semi-automation. This translates to lower operational costs and a better chance to compete in the marketplace.

• Highly efficient and scalable. Digital marketing can easily accommodate a growing number of customers and is capable of responding to their needs in a short span of time. It allows companies to adapt to their needs without having to hire additional personnel.

CONS:

• It requires careful analysis, planning, and should the wrong CRM or Sales Automation Tool be employed, a high level of expertise in IT, e-commerce and customer relationship to be able to function properly.

• Lacks the human aspect which takes into account special cases needing to be addressed. Digital customer engagement treats all customers the same. Of course done right, you micro target and segment to avoid this potential con but it takes more planning and thought and setup.

As it turns out, 'digitizing' customer engagement is not everything. There are certain aspects of customer relationship that could never be replaced by complex machines and IT services. By the same token, relying only on physical customer engagement will yield an equally unpleasant result.

Avoid Both Extremes

Relying on just one mode of customer engagement is a recipe for disaster. There has to be a delicate balance between the two and use them to complement each other. There are many examples of companies that suffered enormously because of their inability to adapt to the changing trends, particularly with the way customers interact with one another and with different businesses institutions.

Tower Records is an example of a business empire that succumbed to the Internet's rise to power. Online music stores slowly ate up their dwindling customer base until its eventual collapse in 2006. A post-mortem analysis showed they failed to compete with other retail and online stores like iTunes that sold digital music and music files at a lower price. Tower Records overstretched their resources in physical stores and outlets and had not come up with the digital alternative in response to the customer's changing needs.

On the other side of the spectrum, Sears Holdings did the exact opposite with the same catastrophic results. Most of its resources had been used up for e-commerce and other online ventures and left a small portion to its brick-and-mortar business. As a result, other companies took up that space and the company lost a substantial amount of market share to its competitors. In just seven years, stock price has gone down by 75%.

We need both to succeed

By now it should be very clear to us that a mixture of digital and physical customer engagement is the key to succeed in a highly competitive environment. Whatever shortcomings digital customer engagement has, is completely wiped out by its physical counterpart, and vice versa.

Be sure you look for a Sales, Marketing and email automation CRM with the ability to handle a combination of social media, phone calls, and emails to succeed. SmallBizDream.com can do that for FREE for up to 2000 communications per month.

STAY IN THE LEAD – KNOW YOUR CUSTOMERS BETTER

More people, millennials especially, are starting their own businesses. Everybody from celebrities, professionals, to working moms and anybody in between. However, without enough resources and the right information to begin with, running any kind of business is guaranteed to be rough-sailing.

Starting a business is never easy, much less running it. There are certain ways you can accelerate your growth if you have the right tools to get the job done. One of the most effective ways to achieve phenomenal growth in any kind of business is by taking a customer-centric approach to marketing and by putting the customers first in day-to-day transactions.

It's All about the Customers

Marketing flops are often the result of not having enough communication between the company and its customers. They assume customers will like a certain kind of product or service when the fact is they want something else. The result is often a totally useless product that completely misses the target market.

To make up for this lapse of judgment, companies will try every trick in the book just to get people to like it. Sometimes they spend millions of dollars on ads and promotional materials to no avail in hopes of salvaging an already precarious situation. At the end of the day, the customers will have their final say and the company will have to face the consequences of not communicating well enough with their customers.

If businesses give customers what they want and creates value for them, customers are going to love them for it and they're going to stay. If all we care about is how we can take advantage of the business opportunity with little or no regard to customer satisfaction, we must stop and rethink our strategy, otherwise we will end up out of business.

Successful business owners put the interest of the customers first. They don't have to beg or chase potential buyers. They show them what they have and provide them with the best products, best customer service, best value for their money, and everything falls naturally into place. Putting the customers first will always pay off in the long run.

Why Businesses Fail

Bloomberg reports in every 10 entrepreneurs 8 will crash and burn within the first 18 months. That's a pretty scary number especially if you haven't got past the 18th month mark.

In a study conducted by Peppers and Rogers Group, 70 percent of the customers leave a company because of poor service and 60 percent fail to convert into customers because they felt customer service was indifferent to their needs.

The reason for failing in most cases is companies glossed over the fact it's their customer service that's been hurting the business. They got too fixated with the numbers at the bottom line and their marketing plan that they often forgot to consider what their customers really thought and felt about them. Sears would be an EXCELLENT example of this.

Some of the most common reasons for business failures which link back to customer service include:

• **Failure to innovate**. Customers can grow tired of having the same old stuff over and over again. They want something fresh and new, perhaps a bit more exciting. If you get stuck with one particular product or style, your customers will probably try out something new from your competitors.

When it comes to marketing strategy, innovation is also key. If you don't have a web portal, a landing page, or a social media account, you've already lost a substantial number of potential customers. The time you stop innovating is the time you start losing ground.

• **Failure to differentiate**. Customers come to you because you offer them something no one else does, or at least something a little bit different. If what you have or offer is all over the place, you'll going have a tough fight ahead of you. Your customers will just as likely go elsewhere as buy from you. Be creative and find your own niche.

• **Failure to communicate.** Perhaps this is the most crucial part and where most companies would either float or sink to the bottom. The majority of traditional outbound marketing practices are just one-way communication. They don't care if you're listening or not; they'll just say what they want you to hear.

Two-way communication is a lot different because you're actively engaged with your customers through customer feedback and the information you get from them would be used as a reference point in improving your goods and services. This can be accomplished by linking up with your customers and potential buyers through social media, spending some time working on your online presence, or providing them with an update about your business on a regular basis. Having a good CRM in place to handle this information for you is very useful.

Having the right skill sets and having the right people doing the job for you is extremely valuable when running any kind of business, and especially dealing with your customers. But not only that, you also need the right kind of tools for your team to be able to work more efficiently.

SALES AUTOMATION AND MARKETING AUTOMATION VS. CUSTOMER RELATIONSHIP MANAGEMENT

What is the difference between Sales, Marketing and Email Automation and Customer Relationship Management(CRM)? Which one is more useful for your business? If you've ever considered all the ways to stay in touch with your customers, I'm sure it's enough to make your head spin.

In the beginning there was much more of a distinction between the two. It was generally believed Customer Relationship Management (CRM) was more about customer service and possibly upselling or reselling new and existing customers, while Sales and Marketing Automation was about the sales cycle and how to prospect and initially sell to new customers or clients.

CRMs were hard to learn and quite expensive so most Small Business owners didn't bother to look at them.

Sales Automation and Marketing Automation tools were often better priced but could only handle ONE or TWO of the necessary functions, which meant you had to purchase multiple tools and figure out how to transfer info between them to make them work together.

I'm going to run down the difference between the two tools so have a better idea what they are, what function they serve and how you can incorporate them into your business.

Customer Relationship Management's (CRM's) main functions were:

- Customer Profile
- Searchable notes and account data on each customer
- Sales History that amalgamates up to departments and the en- tire company
- Tracking of all customer communications
- Customer service tools
- Customer support tools
- Customer retention tools
- Sales campaign tracking and data utilization

Sales Automation and/or Marketing Automation's main functions were:

- Contact Management
- Calendars
- To-do Lists
- Email Automation
- Sales lead assignment and categorization
- Sales Funnel
- Surveys
- Customer Records
- Salesperson tracking and goal and target feedback

Although they seem similar, they have quite different purposes and it can be hard to know which one was traditionally right for you.

They could be used interchangeably but had great overlap, while also being complementary tools.

The great news is today there are many tools that blur the lines even more and can substitute especially for a Small Business (Under $3,000,000/year in sales) For example now you can get software, such as SmallBizDream.com for $29 a month that can handle online funnels you.

No longer do you have to pay thousands of dollars to have these tools. They can actually be quite affordable.

There are some companies that integrate both the sales automation with customer management like Salesforce, HubSpot and Marketo, but for a vast number of small businesses and small shops they are still pricey. For example, HubSpot starts at $200 a month for the very basic package.

Small Business Dream (SmallBizDream.com) can combine the power of Hubspot, Marketo, and Salesforce at no initial cost to you and best of all you can customize to fit your every need.

Here are some of the features you get:

- Contact Management
- Automatic email follow-up
- Calendar integration
- Survey Engine
- Social Media semi-automation tools
- Twitter functionalities
- Sales Funnels
- Business Card Scanning and Transcription service
- Mobile app
- Web App

The last time you bought your groceries, have you noticed something different, like why a certain brand is nearly sold out compared to last week? Conversely, have you noticed other brands just seem to take up space?

This phenomenon is actually a result of what's called predictive analysis. In simple terms, it is a process of trying to know what your customers will likely buy in the future based on the current trends, i.e. what most customers are actually buying today and at what rate.

Now you might think of this as something as simple as, "Okay, my customers liked the carpet cleaner so I will just go out and stack my shelves with a two-month supply." It would be too naïve to think you could easily snatch a fortune by overstocking something your customer already liked. Predictive analysis is more than just that. It demands an awful lot of data gathering, number crunching, decision-making, and some guesswork.

The Role of Customer Relationship Management in Business

Customer Relationship Management tools (CRM) came as a reaction to the rapidly-growing business industry. Back then, we had spreadsheets and repositories to store and analyze data. Now, we have integrated, collaborative software tailored specifically for business use capable of storing unlimited amount of data performing complex calculations, and providing business owners with a comprehensive overview of what is really going on with their business – in real time.

CRM shines in all of these tasks. It is no surprise then that even long-established companies like KFC and McDonalds have been employing CRM tools. It allows CEOs and managers to see the big picture and make sound judgments before calling the shots.

Using CRM to Predict the Future

Making predictions is a tricky business. As stated earlier, you cannot just make decisions based on a particular buying pattern without factoring in specific details like who usually bought them and at what time of the year, quantity, pricing, customer preference, customer service, and the list goes on and on. So how exactly do smart companies make their projections and approximations based on the data from their CRM software?

Every time a customer swipes his or her credit card on the POS counter, information about customer immediately goes to the server where it becomes available for data analysis. Everything from his personal information, items bought, quantity, price, frequency, and date of purchase is channeled down into a vast pool of data. Without the proper tools to analyze and interpret these data, they're nothing more than just a pile of useless names and numbers.

CRM helps business owners by processing this information and transforming the data into something mere humans can understand. This is why loyalty and point cards are so popular with businesses. Your wallet is probably stuffed with them. If you have a loyalty card for your grocery store then the chain store is tracking every purchase you make and putting it into their CRM.

You should narrow down potential customers and repeat customers. The likelihood of a recent customer coming back, can be traced back on what information was made available to the company during the previous transactions. Judging by the customers movement along the trend, the company can make informed decisions to improve their sales. For example, a supermarket owner notices a certain brand of soap gets sold more frequently (and thus more preferred by the customers) than the other. However, the opposite can be said in another store that sells the same product. A good CRM service can help explain this scenario to business owners. In the above example, certain factors like accessibility, pricing, and customer service could be an issue.

A good CRM service keeps track of customers' buying habits, interests, preferences, life- style, and other relevant information about them and constantly updates those data on a regular basis. Factors such as gender, age, occupation, and social status are also key. One of the best ways to maintain a good relationship with your customers is to give something of value to them. Even just a simple email thanking them for making your company a part of their experience will encourage your customers to keep coming back just to return that favor. Guess what? They might even look for other stuff they might be interested in, like handbags or a pair of high-heels to match their cocktail dress they just bought from you.

Keep an eye on past and current trends. Hindsight is said to have a 20/20 vision. CRM takes it a bit further; it actually tells what you should and should NOT be doing based on past and current trends. What was a best-seller might just become a relic in five or ten years . Telecom industries provide a classic example of how changing trends can make or break a company. During the heyday of telecom companies like Nokia, mobile phones were regarded merely as communication devices. New features like apps and media player began to be integrated which essentially turned mobile phones into mini computers. This changed the game dramatically and the once-mighty telecom giant started to wane and fade into obscurity. The moral of the story? Don't ignore the trends. If you haven't struck oil, stop digging. Keep an open mind and try to find what is it that you're missing out.

Smart companies know exactly what to do with their precious load of customer-related data. CRM makes it possible for them to see the forest between the trees and steer the company to the right direction.

Isn't it amazing how even simple Sales, Marketing and Email Automation CRM applications like Small Business Dream can make a big difference to your company? With Small Business Dream you can track your customers and increase your sales.

Why not give it a try for yourself and experience the benefits of employing CRM and sales automation in your small business?

PART VI: LOOKING FORWARD

6 WAYS YOU CAN HIRE THE BIG GUNS

As we talked briefly about in the beginning of this book, hiring new employees is probably the most important aspect of any small business. Most business owners waste a lot of time, money, and energy on finding the right fit for their business. Hiring the wrong person is not only costly, but it devalues your brand as well. According to most recruiters, the cost of a new employee – including your time, training, and benefits – is $240,000. But if you hire the wrong person it can cost you up to $840,000 when you factor in total compensation, including severance, additional hiring, and other disruptions to your business.

Hiring is more than just placing an ad on Craig's List, interviewing, and then checking out references. It's important to have the proper process in place each time a position becomes open.

1) Write Better Job Descriptions

This might seem simplistic, but it is often an overlooked part of hiring. If you don't describe exactly who and what you want, then you'll get the wrong candidates applying for the position. Take some time to really think about the type of person you want to attract. Many companies write detailed descriptions with long lists of responsibilities and requirements; but a study done by the Wall Street Journal says that this can actually alienate a lot of qualified employees.

In the study researchers found in 56 job ads, those that

emphasized what an employer can do for the candidates, found they attracted better quality candidates. Write ads that create excitement and value for the candidate and you'll find the right applicant begging for the job.

2) Interview Multiple Candidates Multiple Times

This may seem intuitive but it's crazy how many people don't take the time to interview more than one candidate. If you let excitement or lack of time get in the way, you're more likely to grasp the first promising lead that comes your way.

You also want to get a second opinion on your candidate. Find either a co-worker or another manager to give your candidate a second opinion, preferably someone with a different personality than you. It is great to see how the candidate does under different circumstances.

3) Focus On Soft Skills

You might be tempted to hire somebody based on work experience and whether they have certain skill sets but social intelligence, institution, conflict resolution, and critical thinking are all skill not easily taught—if at all. When you interview them, evaluate their soft skills. How they interact with you and others. Do they pick up on subtle cues? These should be considered into your decision. Not just an impressive resume.

4) Embrace Social Media

Like most employers, you might do a quick Google search on your candidate and see what comes up online. But you should also be looking through the candidate's social media profiles to check out what sort of person they are. At the very minimum, you should check their LinkedIn profile; but you also want to search them on Facebook and Twitter as well. If you see lots of photographs of parties, then you shouldn't be too surprised if they call in sick on a Monday morning.

5) Improve Your Interview Skills

Sometimes even star candidates don't perform well in interview situations. It's your job to make them feel comfortable and act as naturally as possible. You should think out your interview questions beforehand and roll play with your own staff to make sure you can guide your interviewees to get answers you want. Become a skilled interviewer and you'll find your hiring will improve.

6) Have A Probation Period

When you hire somebody it's best if you make it clear you're hiring them on a trial basis. You never know what issues will pop up. Sometimes you underestimate the chemistry required for an applicant to be successful. Even after you've done all your due diligence you never know if a person will really work out.

Another strategy you can use is to hire your candidate as a free-lancer or an intern. That way if they don't work out then it's not such a big impact. Or if you're desperate for a full-time employee you can give your candidate a small task to complete. For example, you can get them to write a blog article, or do small social media tasks to see how detailed oriented they are.

Hopefully this has given you some helpful tips on how to hire superstars. Hiring top talent will do more than anything to boost your business and take it to the next level.

Now lets get onto the 2nd biggest issue facing Small Business, and this one even affect Micro Business's without staff.

HOW TECHNOLOGY IS CHANGING SALES FOREVER

Technology has shaped the way we do business, especially in the last fifteen years. Over the course of its transformation, the sales and marketing aspect has evolved from one mode of customer engagement to the next. Judging by the rate at which technology catches up with the latest innovations in sales and marketing strategy, we will have to rewrite the rules, leave our old ways, and embrace the future. Sales, Marketing and Email Automation is here to stay and will only evolve.

This paradigm shift has a lot of implications in many of today's small to medium enterprises. As more channels and consumer applications are becoming accessible to a growing number of potential customers, the struggle for customer attention, engagement, and retention will be more relentless than ever.

There are number of ways our recent technological advances in sales and marketing has affected the business sector. However, our focus will be the most prominent ones and have the greatest impact to customer engagement and sales on a global scale.

Shift from traditional marketing to omni-channel marketing. Before PCs and smart phones were adapted for consumer use, customers had no way of interacting with the businesses since everything was basically a one-way communication between the company and the audience (also known as traditional outbound marketing). But as more people are gaining access to online services, this type of customer engagement had slowly become a thing of the past.

Some companies took their old marketing approach and moved it online (YouTube commercials, online ads, online stores, etc.). However, unlike traditional media, online users can air their opinions and comments about the products, services, or the company itself and be read by everyone anywhere in the world. This sparked a new era of customer engagement and the birth of omni-channel marketing.

Businesses are now exploiting the potential of social media, on-line presence, and mobile applications to their fullest and have integrated the latest CRM and Sales and Marketing Automation software to maintain customer relationship and provide sales teams with accurate information about their target market.

This means bigger opportunities for small to medium enterprise. Big companies used to own a large portion of the marketplace until the Internet came along. Their deep pockets enabled them to stay top-of-mind through promotional ventures and ads. Small businesses, on the other hand, couldn't afford to take the same route because they have their whole businesses at stake if things go south.

However, with the major shift from traditional media to online consumerism, this is no longer the case. Today, it is not uncommon to find multi-million-dollar businesses with a solid online presence coming from the lower echelons of the business sector.

Social media, email marketing, content marketing, to name a few, allow business owners to expand their borders far beyond the reaches of traditional marketing, allowing them to secure a large portion of their target market from across the world. These strategies enable their businesses to be within reach to millions of online and mobile users literally at the touch of their fingertips.

However, unlike TV ads and other promotional material, it is by far the most cost-effective method when it comes to promoting brands and maintaining customer loyalty. In fact, it was so effective and economical even long-established companies followed suit and retrofitted their businesses with this kind of marketing strategy

Competition is the natural byproduct of this newfound realm of online customer engagement. During its early stages, the Internet relied heavily in physical servers to create a virtual space for users worldwide.

Cloud computing has effectively wiped out the physical limitations of the cyberspace, creating an infinite world which expands with the growing number of users. This in turn means that our online space has become virtually limitless. Consequently, competing businesses have also grown by the millions using the Internet as the battleground for online supremacy.

To see just how much competition we're talking about, try searching the word 'car' in the Google search bar and you'll find over 5 billion search results just for the word. Assuming you're doing car sales, this meant establishing your online presence would be an uphill battle unless you have the technical know-how to outmaneuver and bury your competitors.

Because competition is so fierce, businesses must continue to innovate and find new ways to stay relevant. Content marketing has become a buzzword and now businesses are flooding the market with blog posts, podcasts and videos. But because there is so much content, it is hard to stand out with a simple 500- word post.

Kijiji featured some up-and-coming rap artists in one of its campaigns. A Montreal rapper made a song called "Gotta sell my stuff" which received over 830,000 views on YouTube. This is the type of content marketing that will be successful, fun, entertaining, and inclusive. Content marketing is not about talking to your customers. It's about including them into the conversation.

Online marketers have devoted their time extensively to this field and devised the most effective methods to gain an edge over the competition. A few good examples are social media marketing, email marketing, and content marketing coupled with a rock-solid Sales, Marketing and Email Automation platform like Small Business Dream, and an e-commerce system to automate most of the tasks.

Improved customer service through CRM and sales automation. Since the advent of Customer Relationship Management tools, customer service has improved by leaps and bounds. Companies doesn't have to make arbitrary decisions or pull numbers out of thin air when trying to figure out their customer's specific 'pain points' or when trying to create value for the customers.

Everything from the customer's personal preferences, buying habits, items bought, down to his last check out are painstakingly stored and analyzed to improve customer experience. As an added feature, platforms like Small Business Dream have integrated a sales funnel into the system, empowering sales team with accurate information and real-time metrics about their leads. On top of this, Small Business Dream also allows companies to sustain their growth with a customer-driven approach emphasizing customer retention. This can be achieved through automated and semi-automated follow-up systems, personalized emails or through social media.

With the current status quo, there's no denying that a small business' only chance for survival is to adapt to the changes brought about by technological advancement. Perhaps you need to improve your online presence or link up with more potential customers through social media or email marketing. There are plenty of CRM applications online which allow you to do just that.

With one last shameless plug, we believe the Free up to 2000 emails or communications per month version of Small Business Dream at SmallBizDream.com is one of the best.

CONCLUSION

Despite the problems I have outlined in this book, I believe the future of small business is very bright.

Regardless of what your customer's needs are, there's one universal way to explode your sales, and keep customer coming back, and/or referring your business to others; Keeping in touch by adding value to your customers. By 'keeping in touch' I'm not saying you should badger your customer incessantly with mindless chatter and sales pitches. By "keeping in touch", you're simply, periodically putting yourself at the forefront of your customer's mind with timely, **helpful**, metered communication.

Now you ask, "what exactly IS timely, helpful, metered communication"?

Well ladies and gentlemen, I'm happy to tell you. Go grab a java, take a seat in a big comfy chair, and read on.

Let's say you're in the real estate business. Obviously, your customers aren't buying real estate the way they'd buy say…socks (or maybe they are). Just because a client makes one real estate purchase doesn't mean the 'sale' is done when your commission check clears, but your client very likely has friends. What do you think happens when those friends are buying property? They ask a friend for a referral. If you position yourself in such a way that there really isn't anyone else your client can think of when asked for that referral, your sales, and therefore your commissions will have no other avenue but to jump exponentially.

Sounds great, right? I mean, who doesn't want to make more

money, while helping a client remember to do helpful things regarding their real estate purchase?

If you could in addition, have those helpful reminders to go out on a set schedule, so much the better, right?

Implementing a simple 'system' for reaching out to those customers automatically makes the task of keeping in touch one of the simpler tasks that you undertake in your business, instead of one you dread for how difficult it can be.

If your business is a restaurant, keeping in touch is even more simple, by sending out 'reminders' of regular specials and special events happening in your establishment. It's easy to keep your income pipeline full, when you're at the forefront of the minds of your customers, regulars or not.

Making the task of staying in touch even simpler, why not implement a mobile Sales and Marketing automation tool to your marketing strategy? That way your business doesn't need to rely on you having time to sit down at a computer to do your 'staying in touch' tasks.

Cool, right?

If you're looking for a way to implement a simple 'stay in touch' system that puts you at the front of your customer's minds, why not grab your free forever for up to 2000 emails or communications per month verson of of Small Business Dream? SmallBizDream.com

Made in the USA
Columbia, SC
02 August 2018